GITTE HASLEBO AND MAJA LOUA HASLEBO

PRACTICING RELATIONAL ETHICS IN ORGANIZATIONS

Taos Tempo Series:
Collaborative Practices for Changing Times

TAOS INSTITUTE PUBLICATIONS
Chagrin Falls, Ohio

PRACTICING RELATIONAL ETHICS IN ORGANIZATIONS

TRANSLATOR: Dorte Herholdt Silver
COVER DESIGN: Kris Harmat

Library of Congress Catalog Card Number: 2011943773

Taos Institute Publications
A Division of the Taos Institute
Chagrin Falls, Ohio
USA

ISBN-10: 0-9819076-8-7
ISBN-13: 978-0-9819076-8-0

Printed in the USA and in the UK

Taos Institute Publications

Publications

The Taos Institute is a nonprofit organization dedicated to the development of social constructionist theory and practice for purposes of world benefit. Constructionist theory and practice locate the source of meaning, value, and action in communicative relations among people. Our major investment is in fostering relational processes that can enhance the welfare of people and the world in which they live. Taos Institute Publications offers contributions to cuttingedge theory and practice in social construction. Our books are designed for scholars, practitioners, students, and the openly curious public. The **Focus Book Series** provides brief introductions and overviews that illuminate theories, concepts, and useful practices. The **Tempo Book Series** is especially dedicated to the general public and to practitioners. The **Books for Professionals Series** provides in-depth works, that focus on recent developments in theory and practice. Our books are particularly relevant to social scientists and to practitioners concerned with individual, family, organizational, community, and societal change.

Kenneth J. Gergen
President, Board of Directors
The Taos Institute

For information about the Taos Institute and social constructionism
visit: www.taosinstitute.net

TAOS INSTITUTE PUBLICATIONS

Taos Tempo Series: Collaborative Practices for Changing Times

Practicing Relational Ethics in Organizations, (2012) by Gitte Haslebo & Maja Loua Haslebo

Relational Leadership: Resources for Developing Reflexive Organizational Practices, (2012) by Carsten Hornstrup, Jesper Loehr-Petersen, Joergen Gjengedal Madsen, Thomas Johansen, & Allan Vinther Jensen

Healing Conversations Now: Enhance Relationships With Elders and Dying Loved Ones, (2011) by Joan W. Chadbourne & Tony Silbert

Riding the Current: How to Deal with the Daily Deluge of Data, (2010) by Madelyn Blair

Ordinary Life Therapy: Experiences from a Collaborative Systemic Practice, (2009) by Carina Håkansson

Mapping Dialogue: Essential Tools for Social Change, (2008) by Marianne "Mille" Bojer, Heiko Roehl, Mariane Knuth-Hollesen, & Colleen Magner

Positive Family Dynamics: Appreciative Inquiry Questions to Bring Out the Best in Families, (2008) by Dawn Cooperrider Dole, Jen Hetzel Silbert, Ada Jo Mann, & Diana Whitney

Focus Book Series

The Appreciative Organization, Revised Edition (2008) by Harlene Anderson, David Cooperrider, Ken Gergen, Mary Gergen, Sheila McNamee, Jane Watkins, & Diana Whitney

Appreciative Inquiry: A Positive Approach to Building Cooperative Capacity, (2005) by Frank Barrett & Ronald Fry

Dynamic Relationships: Unleashing the Power of Appreciative Inquiry in Daily Living, (2005) by Jacqueline Stavros & Cheri B. Torres

Appreciative Sharing of Knowledge: Leveraging Knowledge Management for Strategic Change, (2004) by Tojo Thatchekery

Social Construction: Entering the Dialogue, (2004) by Kenneth J. Gergen, & Mary Gergen

Appreciative Leaders: In the Eye of the Beholder, (2001) edited by Marge Schiller, Bea Mah Holland, & Deanna Riley

Experience AI: A Practitioner's Guide to Integrating Appreciative Inquiry and Experiential Learning, (2001) by Miriam Ricketts & Jim Willis

Books for Professionals Series

New Horizons in Buddhist Psychology: Relational Buddhism For Collaborative Practitioners, (2010) edited by Maurits G.T. Kwee

Positive Approaches to Peacebuilding: A Resource for Innovators, (2010) edited by Cynthia Sampson, Mohammed Abu-Nimer, Claudia Liebler, & Diana Whitney

Social Construction on the Edge: 'Withness'-Thinking & Embodiment, (2010) by John Shotter

Joined Imagination: Writing and Language in Therapy, (2009) by Peggy Penn

Celebrating the Other: A Dialogic Account of Human Nature, (reprint 2008) by Edward Sampson

Conversational Realities Revisited: Life, Language, Body and World, (2008) by John Shotter

Horizons in Buddhist Psychology: Practice, Research and Theory, (2006) edited by Maurits G.T. Kwee, Kenneth J. Gergen, & Fusako Koshikawa

Therapeutic Realities: Collaboration, Oppression and Relational Flow, (2005) by Kenneth J. Gergen

SocioDynamic Counselling: A Practical Guide to Meaning Making, (2004) by R. Vance Peavy

Experiential Exercises in Social Construction – A Fieldbook for Creating Change, (2004) by Robert Cottor, Alan Asher, Judith Levin, & Cindy Weiser

Dialogues About a New Psychology, (2004) by Jan Smedslund

For on-line ordering of books
from Taos Institute Publications visit
www.taosinstitutepublications.net

For further information, call:
1-888-999-TAOS, 1-440-338-6733
Email: info@taosoinstitute.net

CONTENTS >>>

FOREWORD
Kenneth J. Gergen

A few years ago I was deeply upset by a colleague who told me about a failing grade he had given to a young woman. The woman had been the victim of a serious illness and had less than a year to live. Her desperate hope was to complete her university degree before her death. If she passed this particular course, her dreams would be fulfilled; failure meant never achieving her dying wish. From my colleague's standpoint, he was simply carrying out business as usual. If a student didn't achieve a passing mark, a failing grade was the necessary result. Full stop. For me the action was brutally inhumane. I pleaded with him to seek an alternative. In effect, I found the assignment of a failing mark unethical. It was then that I also became aware that indeed the common tradition of assigning grades was not simply a practical matter. It represented an ethical orientation; it was lodged in a longstanding "sense of the good." At the same time, the unreflective assignment of grades was also ethically questionable. When closely examined, then, in our everyday organizational life together, we had a significant ethical dilemma on our hands.

This was an illuminating moment of recognition for me. However, for Gitte Haslebo and Maja Loua Haslebo - the authors of this wonderfully engaging book – the ethical dimensions of everyday life is a major focus of continuing concern. For them, organizational life is not simply composed of activities that are more or less functional in terms of one or more practical ends. Rather, organizational life is suffused with ethical issues; visions of the good are inescapably insinuated into all our otherwise practical activities.

To understand how this is so, Gitte Haslebo and Maja Loua Haslebo develop a compelling view of the organization as a process of active meaning making. As we speak with each other, as we explain our actions, as we tell stories of the organization, we are not only creating the realities we live by, but also a shared sense of the good. In our conversations we are also subtly defining each other - for example, as worthy of respect or admiration – or not. Issues of the good and the worthy are always with us. At the same time, meaning making is in continuous motion, with multiple views of the real and the good often conflicting. The result is that questions of what is good and how should we best behave in the organization are highly complex.

At this point, one might attempt to articulate a series of organizational values, and to examine their particular applications. Indeed, this is the practice of many organizations, striving as they do for values clarification. However, while discussions of organizational values can make a vitalizing contribution to organizational life, the resulting slates of abstract values - "these are the values we stand by" – are largely inconsequential. It is not simply that over time the value statements typically find themselves picking up dust on the shelf. Rather, such values are stated in the abstract, and there is little means of knowing how they apply in any given circumstance. Further, the importance of various values waxes and wanes with time. New values come into prominence (e.g. environmentalism, localism), and earlier commitments no longer seem so relevant. And, forever, there is competition among competing goods. So, very wisely, in my view, the authors steer clear of presenting their own slate of values for organizational life. Rather, they sagaciously return to consider the origin of values and their conflicts, name-ly persons in relationship. The result is a vision of relational ethics, one that sustains the very possibility of ethical action.

Of particular significance, they see within the process of daily conver-sation the grounds for a morally responsive and responsible organization. There are, as they elaborate, ways of talking that generate mutual respect and willingness to cooperate. To be morally responsible in this case is to be responsible to processes of dialogue out of which mutually beneficial forms of life are generated. In effect, the emphasis is on relational responsibility. As they illustrate various moral failures in dialogue, and explain relevant the-oretical ideas, they teach us to reflect on our ways of talking and to exam-ine their consequences. They point the way to effective skills for ethical meaning making.

One comes away from this book realizing that when it comes to ordinary conversation, just "doing what comes naturally" is a potential threat to orga-nizational life. In these simple exchanges we create the organization – for good or ill. Reflection is essential. In the reflections of Gitte Haslebo and Maja Loua Haslebo, we find the path to the good illuminated. For this we should be deeply grateful.

AUTHORS' PREFACE
TO THE ENGLISH EDITION (2012)

This book was published in Danish in 2007. In direct translation, the Danish title was *Ethics in organizations – from good intentions to better possibilities of action.* Our primary intention with the book was to unfold relational ethics in organizations to help shape constructive possibilities of action for members of organizations in difficult situations. The book was well received in Denmark, and we note that some of the concepts we launched have subsequently become more firmly established in management, consultancy and the development of HR methods. This applies especially to the use of the concepts of relational ethics, moral obligations in work communities, bifurcation points, and mutual relatedness within organizations.

This book has become a source of inspiration for reflective managers and consultants and has been included in the curriculum of many educational programs and training courses on management and consultancy work. During the three years since the first edition came out, we have also had the opportunity to discuss the concepts, concerns and messages of the book in an international setting. We have found it particularly rewarding to discuss the perspectives of relational ethics with Peter Lang, Kenneth J. Gergen, Mary Gergen, Sheila McNamee, W. Barnett Pearce, John Winslade, Ilene Wasserman and Jill Freedman– all of them inspirational people whose thinking and work have had a great impact on our consultancy work and writing over the years. In these discussions it was exciting for us to encounter interest and curiosity about the ideas in the book, which were unfortunately inaccessible, as the book was only available in Danish. That led to the idea of having the book translated into English and published by the TAOS Institute. We owe a great debt of gratitude to, especially, Kenneth J. Gergen, Sheila McNamee and Dawn Dole, who have been instrumental in making this possible.

After the decision to translate and publish the book we have abbreviated the Danish book in an attempt to further clarify its key messages. We would like to thank our translator, Dorte H. Silver, who has done a very competent job. We are keenly aware that translation is a demanding task that not only involves comprehensive language skills but also the ability to grasp subtleties of meaning in different cultures. The latter aspect is particularly challenging in a book of this nature, where the key underlying point is the creative powers of language in specific contexts.

The book is written in a Danish setting and influenced by a Scandinavian, democratic approach to management. The nine stories take place in a Danish culture with its underlying assumptions and norms, but we hope that the key features and aspects will be recognizable to an international audience. As the French philosopher Paul Ricoeur (2006) wrote, translation is impossible: The best we can hope for is to become guests in each other's cultures. We hope that readers from other parts of the world will find it interesting and worthwhile to become guests in a Danish culture as they read this book.

One particular challenge in connection with the translation was the many references in the original edition to Danish books and articles that have not been translated into English. Most of these references have been omitted and the points of view explained, but we have left some of them in, as they are simply indispensible.

Another challenge was the translation of words dealing with ethics and moral. The word e*thics* comes from the Greek "ethikos", which stems from "ethos", meaning *custom*. The word *moral*s comes from the Latin word "mos", meaning *mores, customs, manners, morals*. Thus, the original meaning of the two words is very similar. Indeed, the word morals (*moralis*) was coined by Cicero as a translation of the Greek ethikos in his work "De fato" from 44 BCE. In contemporary use the two terms are sometimes used interchangeably. We have chosen, however, to distinguish between them. When we use the word *ethics*, we refer to ideas, principles and reflections on an abstract level as in the naming of ethics theories like the theory of virtue, the theory of duty, the theory of utility – and in our case: relational ethics. When we use the word *moral*, we are addressing dilemmas, choices and actions in everyday life in organizations. In line with this thinking we have chosen this book's title: *Practicing relational ethics in organizations*, thus addressing both reflections and actions.

We hope that this book – in its current English edition – may help build relationships and dialogue across national, cultural and organizational boundaries.

Gitte Haslebo and Maja Loua Haslebo
2012

AUTHORS' PREFACE
TO THE DANISH EDITION (2007)

This book is the result of a lengthy process. For years, it has lived in our thoughts, our conversations and our work as organizational psychology consultants. We are convinced that members of organizations want only the best for themselves and others. Their intentions are good: Managers, consultants and employees all want to help create a meaningful work life that produces important and visible results, and they want to help create a good future for the organization as a whole. In other words, they wish to make constructive contributions and be recognized for their competences – and they are increasingly concerned about achieving this in morally appropriate ways.

Nevertheless, sometimes things go wrong. In surprising ways, events in organizations can lead to loss of face, violations of personal dignity, and damaged relationships. The effects can be far-reaching and detrimental. Managers, consultants and employees spend a great deal of energy on trying to avoid or handle these negative effects, which takes time and energy away from the work at hand. In addition, loss of face or violations of dignity can impair the desire and willingness to communicate, which hampers cooperation. The costs can be so high that members of the organization call in sick, feel compelled to leave the scene and look for work elsewhere, or are dismissed for want of a better solution. Many of these actions can be seen as the result of powerlessness and a sense of having run out of options when the dialogue breaks down, and one is left to face one's doubts, worries and troubling moral concerns alone.

One of the challenges in dealing with moral dilemmas is an inadequate language about moral dilemmas and ethics. In our consultancy work, we have noticed that many organizational members search for words, they can use in their ethical reflections on moral questions. We hope that this book will contribute to building a richer language, a greater vocabulary, and new navigational tools that members of organizations can use to address moral dilemmas. A richer language for dealing with morality and ethics is a matter of giving new life to familiar terms and conceiving new key terms and concepts. In this book we will strive to bring these terms and concepts to life by applying them in relation to nine stories which we have collected over the years. The stories illustrate how morality and ethical considerations are embedded in all our actions in organizations, and how we can enhance our awareness to particularly important bifurcation points where one's choice of words and actions can have decisive influence on whether we affect our social world for the better or for the worse. In the stories, for the sake of anonymity, we have altered the participants' names as well as certain factual information that does not affect the understanding or the point of the story.

This book is mainly intended for managers, consultants and employees who are interested in the moral and ethical aspects of everyday events in organizations, and who wish to learn how they can help improve conditions and results in the work community. The book will also be relevant for students with an interest in communication, organizational psychology, ethics, management, human resource development, and organizational development.

We would like to thank our colleagues and partners, as well as our customers and participants in training courses. These collaborations have given us a rich source of inspiration for developing new ideas, incorporating important issues, and defining the overall themes of the book. Through these relationships we have learned about the many moral dilemmas that preoccupy organizational members. While incorporating a wide range of concepts and ideas, this book also has a strong experiential basis as we share our own and others' experiences with navigating in complexity and unpredictability guided by a desire to help construct a better social world. This interest is shared by many managers, consultants and employees who want to discover how relational and more respectful methods can be used to create improved possibilities of action and better results in organizations.

We would like to thank everyone who has taken the time to discuss the topics of the book with us or offered feedback on the first drafts of chapters. In particular, this includes Peter Lang, Jane Palm, Ulla Andersen, Flemming Andersen, Peter Hansen-Skovmoes, Lone Clausen, Karen Faurfelt, Michala Schnoor, Katrine Bastian Meiner, Povl Dolleris Røjkjær, Mette Borg Jensen, Britta Gerd Hansen and Troels Østergaard Jørgensen. We are also very grateful to the managers, consultants and employees who have contributed with stories, and who have spent time and effort letting us interview them and later reviewing our narrative summaries of their experiences. These contributions have been crucial for our ability to connect ideas, assumptions and models from the abstract world with the complexities of concrete everyday life, where many actors' thoughts and actions are interwoven to create the social world that becomes our reality.

We would also like to thank our publisher, Dansk psykologisk Forlag, where Editors Marianne Kølle and Lone Berg Jensen have provided highly professional feedback – and sometimes very challenging comments – as this book came together. Their belief in this project and support along the way has been of great value to us.

Gitte Haslebo and Maja Loua Haslebo
June 2007

LIST OF STORIES ON
MORAL DILEMMAS IN ORGANIZATIONS

LIST OF FIGURES

CHAPTER 1:

WHY RELATIONAL ETHICS?

Sometimes people in organizations experience humiliation, hurt and disrespect. It is our firm conviction that this is not a result of bad intentions but instead an unintended effect of vague ethics theories and inadequate navigational tools when organizational members find themselves in moral dilemmas. We are convinced that relational ethics will be of great value and use with respect to creating better social worlds in organizations and in society.

In our experience, managers, consultants and employees are increasingly concerned with moral questions such as "What should I do in this difficult situation?", "How can I face myself if I respond in kind?", "How do I decide between options A and B, when it seems like a choice between a rock and a hard place?", "How do I implement this tough decision with the least amount of damage?" or "How can I act sensibly when a colleague disregards my points of view and ridicules me?"

These examples describe situations in which one has time to pause and ponder on a moral question – with oneself and maybe others. However, many everyday situations unfold so quickly that we act without much thought. We operate on autopilot and pick what seems like the only available option. In a common-sense moral order we tend to be directed by righteous indignation and to award ourselves the right to assess the moral quality of other people's actions without much consideration for the context that they occur in. In common-sense morality, we often see the world in black and white, opposites, conflicts, and good versus bad, and we hold each other to account, make others see the error of their ways, assign guilt and blame – all in the hope of making other people wiser and better human beings. In theory, the logic may seem strong, but unfortunately it does not work that way in practice. Instead common-sense morality, moral indignation and assignment of guilt and blame damage relationships, create separateness, and narrow our scope of possible actions. What, then, do we do? What paths can we take to rise above everyday judgmental morality?

One possibility might be to turn to classic ethics theories, such as virtue ethics or the ethics of duty, which offer universal guidelines and categorical requirements for moral behavior. These ethics theories are an integrated feature of Western culture and part of the basis for the ethical reflections of organizational members. However, as these theories are universal and categorical, they do not serve as helpful tools in specific and difficult situations. There will always be too many exceptions to the rules in the shape of particular circumstances and complicating details. Therefore there is a need for concepts and navigational tools that will assist organizational members in unique situations, which can be understood in different ways and often involve many conflicting considerations.

Another approach – besides the classic ethics theories – is to rely on one's gut feeling and intuition. When we find ourselves in a moral dilemma and are unable to find rational reasons for choosing either A or B, eventually we often rely on what feels right and argue that "I did this because it just felt like the right thing to do." We cannot explain in words why we did what we did. This ethics approach is related to the notion of remaining authentic (true to our feelings), open (sharing our feelings) and honest (telling the truth about our feelings). These particular ethical values are often at play in organizations. When authenticity, openness and honesty are high on the agenda, conversations risk becoming less than constructive and perhaps even downright destructive: "I'm just saying this in the interest of being open" and "Well, to be quite honest ..." are phrases that often precede damaging criticism of a colleague's actions or personality. The idea of relying on subjective gut feelings as the basis for a moral choice springs from the assumption that there is a truth and that this can be found in the mind of the individual. Based on both theory and our practice as organizational psychology consultants we consider this path to be counterproductive as it serves to divide organizational members and tempts them to reserve the right to view the world in one particular perspective: their own limited point of view.

In our work as organizational psychologists and in our writings, we have thus chosen to develop a third path, which we call *relational ethics*. Taking this path requires abandoning the universal definitions of true and false, good and bad, right and wrong and turning instead to an emphasis on co-construction of meaning, coordination of actions and mutual relatedness among organizational members.

In this book, we focus on unfolding relational ethics in an organizational setting, although we are convinced that the use of relational ethics might help create a better social world in many other settings: in international negotiations, the media, our education system, family life, etc. We view organizations as work communities where moral obligations and entitlements are defined in part by the membership of the organization.

Essentially, organizations contain both common and conflicting interests and perspectives, and access to influence is not evenly distributed. We are also concerned with the link between ethics on the one hand and results and organizational efficacy on the other, and we do not consider it relevant to ask *whether* a particular company can afford to work with ethics right now. On the contrary, we are convinced that ignoring the many moral and ethical aspects of everyday events has a strong negative impact on the bottom line. As illustrated by the nine stories in this book, the loss of personal dignity and lack of appreciation can mean that much work time is spent repairing dignity and damaged relationships. Therefore, we believe that all organizations at all times must deal carefully with moral questions. No organization can afford not to.

The purpose of the book is not to make everyday life in organizations simpler or more predictable. Rather we wish to inspire the readers to embrace complexity, changeability and unpredictability and to acknowledge their own capacity for doing this. The book does not provide a list of correct answers. We do not intend to provide tools for managing and controlling events or for reducing unpredictability. There is already an abundance of books that aspire to do this. Since complexity and unpredictability are general conditions of everyday life for all of us, it may be more helpful to heighten our awareness of our own role in the events that unfold and of the situations and outcomes we are involved in creating. To think that we can control events would be an illusion, but giving up and trying to stay out of events implies a neglect of responsibility. Neither is desirable. Instead, we hope to steer a middle course: to see our own role and contributions and to create and choose possible actions based on an awareness of the concerns we ought to show other members of our work community.

To illustrate how moral issues and ethics are embedded in all our daily actions in organizations we tell nine stories from life in organizations. Some of these stories will seem quite recognizable and thus help us demonstrate how everyday events contain both practical wisdom and challenging moral issues. Other stories are very dramatic. The first time we heard them, they seemed hard to believe, and we discussed how real life exceeded our imagination. Nevertheless, they are actual stories from everyday life in organizations. Each of the stories is told by a manager, an employee or a consultant. The stories are personal tales about events, in which one or more of the persons experienced doubts or moral dilemmas and found it hard to see a constructive way forward. In our use of the stories we entertain a variety of ideas, interpretations and possibilities of action as they might appear from the perspectives of the narrator and other actors. Thus, we introduce additional hypothetical voices. Using a hypothetical language lets us play out a variety of possible ways for the actors in a given story to attribute meaning to the events and move on. The hypothetical language springs from the awareness that events in organizations are unpredictable and open to multiple interpretations, and that any utterance and any action can lead in many different directions. We also attempt to use a dialogic approach in our writing, inviting the reader to enter into the various and often conflicting ethical considerations that we discuss. We try to write in a way that lets our readers discover all the practical wisdom that they already possess. By practical wisdom we mean the skilled capacity to coordinate our actions with those of others in a changing world – without necessarily understanding what goes on in another person's mind.

We have found inspiration in linguistic philosophy, moral philosophy, ethics theory, sociology, social psychology, organizational theory, management theory, psychology, anthropology, and communication theory. In our presentation of key concepts, we strive to include the context in which the ideas were developed. This effort has involved a far-ranging search for concepts, ideas, models and approaches that might help us explore and unfold what ethical reflections on moral issues might involve. We aim to present other authors' theoretical contributions briefly yet loyally. However, this is not in any traditional sense an academic book with in-depth criticism of shortcomings and inconsistencies in other authors' contributions. We choose to focus mainly on those authors whose contributions we find particularly relevant and useful in relation to the topics of the book. The book should also serve as a guide for the reader in the field of a very extensive literature, while we as authors clearly indicate when we take over and seek to further develop the concepts and make them useful in an organizational setting.

Choice of possible actions should be guided by an awareness of the – often implicit – assumptions about people, organizations, learning, change, development, etc. In this book we seek to make these implicit assumptions explicit – both with regard to making sense of everyday events in organizations and with regard to HR methods and tools. Insight into these assumptions is a prerequisite for choosing appropriate actions and methods. Any possible action and any method are anchored in a theory and an epistemology that rests on certain assumptions. Essentially, choosing tools for organizational development means choosing an epistemology and thus also ways to influence and thereby to obtain potential consequences. Thus, the book may also serve as a guideline for managers and HR consultants who are responsible for choosing among a wide range of methods, tools and external consultants.

To us, drawing on the complexity, ambiguity, fluidity and unpredictability of everyday life means abandoning the notion that actions of organizational members can be planned and steered in predetermined directions. It also means abandoning the notion that committing plans to paper increases the likelihood that managers and employees will actually carry out the plans. In other words, we have to abandon the current planning and control rationale, where even personal development is put into a schedule, subjected to scaled ratings and implemented like a military operation with painstakingly developed objectives and phases.

In Chapter 2 we offer an introduction to epistemology and compare the key assumptions in realism and social constructionism. We also unfold seven basic assumptions that spring from social constructionism and demonstrate how social constructionism is related to relational ethics.

In each of the following five chapters we address a key concept from social constructionism and show how the concept can be used to shed light on the co-creation of meaning, the coordination of actions, and the mutual relatedness in organizations. The five concepts are: context, relationship, discourse, appreciation, and power. It is our conviction that these five concepts can offer a fruitful and helpful basis for discovering the moral compass points that make up a relational ethics.

In Chapter 3 we address the concept of context. By context we mean the meaning-constructing pattern within which events unfold. *Context* is not simply something that "is", or which we are "exposed to", but rather something that is created through language. In order to grasp what this means we open with a philosophical discussion of language. In analyses that are based on common-sense understanding and realism, language is treated as a means of describing a pre-existing reality. Social constructionism instead focuses on the creative powers of language and how we use language to affirm or alter the social world that we experience as our reality. We review some of the main contributions from the linguistic philosophers Ludwig Wittgenstein and John Austin. Next, we turn to W. Barnett Pearce's social constructionist perspective of communication and illustrate how meaning is constructed through speech acts and episodes. In organizations, meaning is created in unpredictable and uncontrollable ways that no single individual can grasp in its full extent. The exploration of the concept of context leads to a moral obligation, which we call social responsibility. When we assume social responsibility we embrace the idea that we are not simply subjected to events but co-creators and thus co-responsible for constructing situations in which all involved can contribute constructively.

In Chapter 4 we take a close look at the concept of relationships. Realism and social constructionism both focus on the importance of relationships, but there are some key differences between the two points of view. In this chapter we discuss how relational thinking varies with epistemology. Here too, we draw inspiration from the linguistic philosopher John Austin, who sheds light on the relation-building power of language and on the embeddedness of moral obligations and entitlements in language. Next, we turn to examples from narrative-inspired anthropological research that explores how words take their meaning from the cultural context. Our interest in the relation-building power of language leads to the moral compass point that we call the obligation to engage in dialogue.

In Chapter 5 we turn to discourses and narratives. We discuss how historically and culturally shaped discourses deliver material for living stories in organizations. A narrative perspective on stories about events in organizations makes it clear that the narrative plot defines positions and determines how organizational members are assigned certain positions rather than others and thereby are attributed "personal traits". In this chapter we review discourses that are common in many organizations, such as the discourse on change management, the discourse on individual dysfunction, diagnosis and treatment, and the discourse on documentation and evaluation. Discourses and narratives offer a limited number of positions. The positioning of managers and employees determines their moral obligations and entitlements. This chapter illustrates the creative powers of discourses and stories. When, for example, stories involving villain and victim positions become dominant in an organization, the moral obligations and entitlements are defined in ways that are hard for the individual organizational member to escape. In Chapter 5 we demonstrate how discourses and stories that shape subject-object relationships are not helpful in creating a better social world. The narrative angle on events encourages us to listen in a discursive manner, that is, to pay attention to the positions we place ourselves and others into and to assume a shared responsibility for ensuring a positioning that shapes mutually respectful relationships and makes dialogue possible.

In Chapter 6, the focus is on recognition and appreciation. Initially, we discuss John Dewey's ideas on exploration as experiential learning, change, participatory knowledge and moral education. John Dewey was an important source of inspiration for the development of both the CMM theory

(Coordinated Management of Meaning) and Appreciative Inquiry. We also include the German philosopher and social critic Axel Honneth, who has written seminal works on various forms of recognition, as his ideas may provide inspiration for a further development of the use of Appreciative Inquiry in organizations. Next, we illustrate how Appreciative Inquiry can serve as a valuable alternative to traditional problem-solving approaches in organizations. We unfold the basic assumptions about learning, change and development and illustrate the link between these assumptions and ethics. Appreciative Inquiry leads to a moral obligation, which we call inquiry of value to the work community. It is not sufficient to consider and reflect on a situation based on realism. In a social constructionist perspective, it is important to include thinking about how one's own and others' positions and actions can be of value to the entire work community.

In Chapter 7, the focus is on power. Organizational members do not have the same opportunities for making their voices heard, shaping constructive contexts and assuming moral obligations in accordance with a relational ethics. This chapter draws on ideas by the French philosopher Michel Foucault to explore the role of traditional and modern power in organizations. Next, we turn to the Australian therapist Michael White, who has explored modern power and normalizing judgment. The chapter introduces the moral obligation of helping to create a scope of possibilities where managers and employees can interact as morally responsible and reliable individuals who enter into mutually respectful relationships.

The closing chapter of the book gathers up the many threads we have spun and demonstrates how moral obligations and entitlements are interwoven and combine to form the content of relational ethics. A pattern emerges that may serve as a source of inspiration both in making constructive contributions in the everyday flow of events in organizations and in developing new HR methods appropriate for strengthening teamwork, work quality, creativity, and the organization's overall results.

CHAPTER 2

SOCIAL CONSTRUCTION
AND RELATIONAL ETHICS

In this chapter we offer a brief introduction to the idea of social constructionism and a comparison between realism and social constructionism as
two very different ways of approaching the world and the organization.
Next, we point to what we consider seven key social constructionist assumptions and exemplify how they can be used in practice in organizations.
Furthermore, we illustrate what these assumptions mean to us personally as
consultants and in relation to the moral challenges we encounter in our consultancy work. We hope that these reflections can serve as inspiration for
managers, employees and consultants.

Theory and practice are related. When we act we rely on ideas about how
the world works. Behind every tool and every method lie assumptions about
the world, learning and development, and human beings. These assumptions
are often unspoken – we take them so much for granted that we think we
know how it is. Therefore, we cannot always see how our practice is related to
theory. Sets of basic assumptions are called epistemologies, that is, theories
about how we conceive or come to know something. Epistemology is the
basis of theory, which in turn inspires practice. Any organizational member
has ideas about the world and acts accordingly. Thus, every organizational
member deals with epistemology, theory and practice. In the context of this

book, the main point to note is how profoundly interactions in the organization are affected by the assumptions on which organizational members rely.

In the words of Peter Lang, who was associated with the former Kensington Consultation Centre in London: "People can be very passionate about theories" – a comment from personal conversation that gives food for thought, evoking images of discussions about change, learning, development, etc. where emotions run high, cheeks are flushed, and voices are raised. But why are we so passionate about theories? Perhaps because theories spring from an explicit or implicit epistemology that is closely associated with personal values. Thus, it is not an abstract philosophical question or a purely technical issue to choose the words, concepts and models we rely on. It is also a matter of how we view our professional identity and the relationships we wish to build with customers, colleagues, business partners, etc.

Social constructionism is not a clearly defined paradigm or school of thought but a diverse collection of ideas, concepts and perspectives based on contributions from many theorists and practitioners. Kenneth J. Gergen and Mary Gergen deserve mention as some of the earliest proponents as well as the most prolific. Already in the 1980s Kenneth J. Gergen, professor of psychology at Swarthmore University, published his ideas about how people construct their understanding of reality (see for example Gergen, 1985). The major treatise *Realities and Relationships* by Gergen was published in 1994, and in 2004 Kenneth J. Gergen and Mary Gergen, who is also a Professor of Psychology, published a condensed presentation of the ideas in social constructionism: *Social Construction – Entering the Dialogue* (Gergen & Gergen, 2004).

The development of social constructionism was based on a critique of the prevailing paradigm in the human sciences known as positivism, empiricism or realism (Burr, 1995). Essentially, epistemology concerns convictions about what it takes for us to think that we understand something. Under what circumstances can we trust our assumptions – about what is real, rational, or good? What thoughts do we have about the way in which knowledge is created? Realism and social constructionism offer very different answers to these questions.

REALISM AND SOCIAL CONSTRUCTIONISM

Realism presumes the existence of an exterior world the properties of which are independent of the observer's thoughts and perceptions. Realism rests on the conviction that it is possible to describe "things out there" and their characteristics and workings in an objective and unambiguous way. The purpose of scientific methods is to uncover and describe universal regularities that define the link between cause and effect. Within the framework of this epistemology it is assumed that we can only achieve true understanding if we know the cause or causes of the phenomena we are studying. Scientific development is linked to a belief in progress: Stringent research methods are presumed to be able to bring us closer to a correct and adequate description of objective reality. The goal is to define universal regularities accurately enough that we can predict future events. In the attempt to uncover universal regularities it is essential to keep observations and studies free from the researcher's subjective assessments or preconceived notions. Researchers should adopt a neutral stance and strive to leave themselves out of the equation.

Social constructionism is a distinctly different epistemology, which abandons the idea of being able to arrive at an unambiguous and correct description of any objective reality: *"The foundational idea of social construction seems sim-*

ple enough, but it is also profound. Everything we consider real is socially constructed. Or, more dramatically: Nothing is real unless people agree that it is. Your skeptical voice might respond, 'You mean that death is not real', or 'the body,' or 'the sun,' or 'this chair' …and the list goes on. We must be clear on this point. Social constructionists do not say, 'There is nothing,' Or 'There is no reality.' The important point is that whenever people define what 'reality' is, they are always speaking from a cultural tradition" (Gergen & Gergen, 2004, pp.10-11).

Figure 1

Key Assumptions in Realism and Social Constructionism

REALISM	SOCIAL CONSTRUCTIONISM
Objective and universal knowledge and truth	Historically and culturally shaped knowledge
Science can uncover reality	Science deals with what certain groups of researchers agree to define as valid knowledge
Language describes reality	Language creates our understanding of reality
Neutral observation is possible	Any observation is made from a particular vantage point
The individual comes before the relationship	The relationship comes before the individual
Clarity	Ambiguity
Focus on "how things are"	Focus on "how things ought to be"
Values: truth and predictability	Values: co-creation and social responsibility

Social constructionism has been under development for more than 40 years and has served as a rich source for the development of a wide range of practice fields, e.g. in therapy, mediation and organizational consultation.

Choice of epistemology greatly influences the way organizational members think and act in organizations. David Cooperrider is one of the pioneers applying social constructionist ideas and concepts to practice in organizations. In 1987 he co-wrote the article *Appreciative Inquiry in Organizational life* together with Suresh Srivasta, which was to have a groundbreaking impact on innovation in organizations. Cooperrider builds on Gergen's ideas about reality as a social construction. David Campbell has also offered useful contributions to understand how social constructionist assumptions can be helpful in organizations – especially in the book *The Socially Constructed Organization* (Campbell, 2000). From Denmark there is, for example, *Systems and Meaning. Consulting in Organizations* (Haslebo & Nielsen, 2000). Another widely used Danish book, which has been published in Danish only, applies social constructionist concepts in an organizational context (Haslebo, 2004).

In the following section we offer seven key assumptions in social constructionism as an initial introduction. In the remainder of the book we will unfold, specify, explore and demonstrate the complexity of these assumptions in an attempt to field concepts and ideas that can aid our understanding of moral challenges in organizations and, facilitate useful possibilities of action for organizational members.

SOCIAL CONSTRUCTIONIST ASSUMPTIONS
IN AN ORGANIZATIONAL SETTING

An epistemology consists of *assumptions about knowledge* and about *what it takes for us to make sense*. These assumptions carry large portions of our culture, are embedded in our education and upbringing, and over time become so familiar to us that we understand them as truths: elements in our world that we know and come to rely on. Assumptions are associated with cultural and personal values, and in some cases they are integrated in our self-conception. For example, one assumption stemming from realism is the existence of truth and lie. This assumption is so firmly rooted and widespread in Western culture that many of us incorporate it into our self-image and prefer to see ourselves as honest individuals who rarely lie. This example also illustrates the link between epistemology, ethics and moral obligations. The assumption of truth versus lie is connected with the moral obligation that we should tell the truth and refrain from lying. Thus, choosing to act on the basis of one epistemology rather than another is very much a *moral* choice. In the following review of the seven key assumptions in social constructionism we aim to clarify the connections between social constructionism and relational ethics.

1. Organizational Members construct their Reality by Means of the Language they use

From a social constructionist perspective it is not possible to describe an organization as it truly *"is"*. There are no unambiguous answers as to the characteristics of a particular organization. This idea contradicts our common-sense everyday experience where we seem to register soberly that the organization is doing well against the competition, that the working climate has deteriorated in recent months, or that the new head of the department is incompetent. From a social constructionist point of view, however, these conclusions about the organizational 'reality' are not merely sober observations but powerful conceptions that are created and intensified by the language that the organizational members choose to use. Thus, the key question is not what characterizes the organization, the situation or the problem but how organizational members manage to form the understandings that guide their actions.

This approach has profound implications for the way in which managers, employees or consultants relate to the events they are a part of and for the questions they ask in order to learn more about their own and other people's understandings and possibilities of action.

As consultants in an initial consultation with the purpose of clarifying a potential consultancy assignment, we do not ask, "What is the core of your problem?" or "What is the cause of the conflict between departments A and B?" Both questions spring from the epistemology of realism and invite the persons being present in the meeting to engage in a line of thinking which presupposes that reality can be described unambiguously and objectively. Instead we might ask, "How would you as a manager describe this problem, and how do various staff groups talk about it?" or "How have you as a member of this management team come to view the events as a conflict?" Thus, our focus is on the ways in which understandings are created, recreated and reshaped in the organization.

Thus, choosing social constructionism as one's basis means abandoning the notion of a clear distinction between an objective (real) and a subjective (mental) world. It also means abandoning the notion that language can be used as a precise and reliable link between the two. The function of language is conceived quite differently in social constructionism than it is in common-sense understanding and realism, both of which assume that language reflects an objective reality and that it can be used to describe, uncover and explain causal links underlying phenomena "out there" in a clear and unambiguous way.

From a social constructionist perspective, language is not a passive, neutral mirror. The language we use in interaction is instead an active tool for creating the reality that we instantly experience as *"right there in front of us"*. We produce reality through language. For example, if organizational members spend a great deal of time talking about how age seems to unfairly determine who gets the interesting assignments, and how younger staff members are shortchanged, that produces a reality in the organization that involves a greater focus on age differences compared to other types of differences such as experience, education, seniority, etc. Conversations that focus on age provide legitimacy to one distinction among many possible distinctions. Topics that are legitimized attract greater attention, and events that are associated with these topics are selected and remembered more clearly and for longer. Thus, the language we use contains a *self-fulfilling prophecy*: We predict something which we then subsequently bring about, and thus, the prediction seems to have been proven true. When an investigation is launched into the causes of a poor psychological working climate, organizational members will develop associated concepts and terminology and notice incidents that they see as examples of a poor psychological climate. Thus, the poor psychological climate and its potential causes become prominent features in the organization.

Language is also open to multiple interpretations and variation over time. A single word cannot be defined in itself but gets a meaning from the context it is embedded in and the community of practice that uses it. For example, when managers and employees debate why they have such a poor psychological climate at work, they may appear to be talking about the same. However, a few exploratory questions will most likely reveal that they associate given concepts with different experiences and stories. Each community of practice will have its own version of what a poor psychological climate is all about.

The assumption that language shapes our understanding of reality means that managers, employees and consultants cannot use language as a "free" means of gathering information or uncovering the "actual" roots of a problem. This impossibility of using language "for free" implies that we cannot make a statement or pose a question without affecting each other and our relationships. If a manager asks a staff member at a meeting why he or she did not hand in a scheduled report on time, that is not a "free" request for information but an act that may have small or large repercussions for the staff member in question and his or her self-conception, reputation and possibilities of working with others.

The assumption that our language use actively creates the reality we live in, implies that our use of different words and angles would give rise to a different reality. Thus, all change begins with language.

Hence it is a major moral challenge to pay attention to the language we use in specific situations. Language can serve to intensify or tone down a conflict. Language can be hostile and damage relationships. Language can be appreciative and facilitate communication and dialogue. Our language use is a matter of choice. In any given situation we can choose from a wide range of expressions, and thus we have a choice and a shared responsibility for co-creating a better social world.

A social constructionist vantage point invites our commitment to engage in inquiry into the ways in which understanding is created in an organization. It encourages an irreverent exploration of how our own thoughts and hypotheses affect what we focus on, and where we direct our attention as managers, consultants and employees. As the utterances we make and the questions we ask play a role in creating the social reality we are a part of, every utterance is a moral choice. The moral aspect first of all requires us to consider whether the question we are about to ask will help create a better social world, and secondly it requires us to take responsibility for our choice of phrasing. A question to a manager who feels that a coworker is chiding him or her might be, "Why don't you just tell him to shut up?" Would that particular question help create a better social world? Probably not. Therefore, it is necessary to choose a different wording. In this case, a social constructionist approach might involve entertaining many different thoughts and possible actions and considering their likely consequences.

2. An Organization can be understood as an Arena for varying Communities of Practice

The individual manager or employee is a member of multiple communities of practice in and outside the organization. In this book we are mainly interested in communities of practice (for instance a department, a team or a specific professional group) within organizations, but we are well aware that the full range is far wider. Each community of practice can be seen as a relational network consisting of agents who communicate with each other and thus build a common understanding of the organization, its past, present and future, everyday events, current problems and opportunities, etc.

Instead of viewing an organization as an object that has a stable character and can be described by means of numbers, organizational charts, business strategies, HR policies, etc., a social constructionist perspective involves seeing a dynamic and continually changing organizing of varying communities of practice that organizational members join and leave in somewhat chaotic and unpredictable ways over time, and which deal with varying themes over time. For example, the theme in a community of practice during the early stages of a merger may be phrased as "How do we avoid being swallowed up by the others?" and later turn into "How do we demonstrate to the others what our particular strong points are?"

A view of shifting communities of practice stimulates our awareness of and curiosity toward change, ambiguity, transient formations of meaning, and unpredictability. For managers, consultants and employees, therefore, it is important to pay attention to the relational networks that are part of the various communities of practice as well as the emergence of partially conflicting versions of reality. From this point of view it becomes clear that individual organizational members cannot simply speak with one voice but must speak with as many voices as the number of the communities of practice to which they belong.

To us as consultants, this assumption is a reminder to steer clear of discussions between communities of practice concerning who has the correct or the most adequate understanding. At the same time it gives us the moral obligation to help all communities of practice get a voice and be heard in the conversations and discussions that take place in the organization. It is also important to award organizational members a range of legitimate voices corresponding to the various communities of practice to which they belong.

3. Discourses and Narratives incorporate Organizational Members' Experiences into a Holistic Understanding

How do we make sense of the myriad events and actions, thoughts and feelings that we experience on a daily basis in the organizations of which we are a member? From a social constructionist perspective, our self-conception in relation to others is essentially organized as a narrative, that is, a story. Fragments of impressions, experiences and our own and others' utterances are not meaningful in themselves but are attributed meaning depending on the narratives into which they are incorporated. Many fragments fail to find a place in an ongoing narrative and are thus neither noticed nor remembered. That means that by structuring experiences into narratives we create a holistic understanding of the events that unfold over time.

One of the important contributors to this understanding is Jerome Bruner, who, in his book *Acts of Meaning,* describes his goal of developing a folk psychology or a cultural psychology. *"Rather, it is an effort to illustrate what a psychology looks like when it concerns itself centrally with meaning, how it inevitably becomes a cultural psychology and how it must venture beyond the conventional aims of positivist science with its ideals of reductionism, causal explanation and prediction"* (Bruner, 1990, pp. xii-xiii).

This social constructionist assumption forms the basis of the narrative approach, which offers a different answer than realism to the fundamental epistemological question, "What does it take for us to make sense?" In the terms of positivist science (realism) the answer would be, "Break the phenomenon down to its components, examine causal relations between them, and describe these relations as regularities that enable reliable predictions." By contrast, a social constructionist answer would be, "We achieve understanding when we are able to combine fragments of experiences into a coherent narrative that involves ourselves along with others – a story that has a past, a present and a future".

A story involves a narrator and an audience. The story involves various actors who act in relation to each other and in ways that make sense within the framework of the plot. The story has an underlying theme that provides meaning for the developing plot. A story has a moral message that is established gradually or appears as a surprise element at the end.

In the narrative approach reductionism is replaced by holistic understanding; causal explanations are replaced by morally founded explanations of the actors' actions; and predictability is replaced by fluidity and unpredictability.

A story is not a well-defined, clear-cut presentation but is told differently depending on the context and the audience. A manager's story about "the time when I was hired and only later discovered that my predecessor had been sacked," will be framed differently whether it is told to close friends, a new employee (if he or she even gets to hear the story) or a network of managers from other organizations. The narrative approach does not imply that the story exists in a finite form in the narrator's mind, so that only the language is adjusted to the circumstances; the idea is rather that the story is reshaped by the narrator and the audience within a given context.

Any organization is home to a wealth of narratives. Some of them spring from the discourses that are part of our common cultural heritage. One of these narratives is the discourse on the necessity of personal development as the means of becoming a well-functioning organizational member. This discourse is so widespread and so dominant in the Western culture that we take its underlying assumptions for granted. In Chapter 5 we review some of the discourses that influence the planning of learning and development activities in organizations.

4. The Individual Organizational Members' Selves are shaped in the Relationships and Communities of Practice in which the Members Participate

One of Kenneth J. Gergen's major contributions is his role in developing new ideas about individuals and relationships. In his seminal work *Realities and Relationships* he writes, *"Many scholars welcome constructionism because it challenges the 'cult' of the individual that is endemic to Western tradition. As the implications of a communal or relational ontology are developed, however, many also find the deemphasis on psychological processes unsettling. It places secure and trusted beliefs about persons, including ourselves, into question. The 'individual mind' loses not only its ontological grounding but all of its traditional constituents – the emotions, rational thoughts, motives, personality traits, intentions, memory, and the like. All these constituents of the self become historically contingent constructions of culture"* (Gergen, 1994, pp. 69-70).

In a social constructionist perspective, our view of ourselves and our identity stems from *"a relational view of self-conception, one that views self-conception not as an individual's personal and private cognitive structure but as discourse about the self — the performance of languages available in the public sphere"* (Gergen, 1994, p. 185). In organizations managers and employees construct meaning in their work life and relationships with other organizational members through the stories they tell. The stories that are told include embedded narratives about the narrator's self. The individual organizational members have a certain number of stories available about themselves. Which stories can be told where, and when, depends in part on which communities of practice the organizational member belongs to.

The idea that an individual has many "selves" or ways of understanding him/herself as a manager or an employee may seem provoking. It is a notion that lies far from our common-sense understanding and the traditional individualist perspective in psychology with its focus on the individual's true and firm "inner core". From this perspective an obvious question would be, "But how does the individual organizational member choose which self to display in any given situation?" A social constructionist answer would consist of two parts. First, we have to abandon the notion of the individual as an autonomous being who decides, in isolation, to *be* in a certain way. Thus, the question might be rephrased: "Under what circumstances can an organizational member enact his or her various selves?" Here, interactions with others are crucial. A manager or a staff member "is" not unambiguously or invariably someone who "is" decisive, helpful, creative, dynamic, etc. but rather someone who — depending on the given context and community of practice — gets certain opportunities to present him/herself and to be recognized by others as decisive, helpful, creative, dynamic, etc. — or something else entirely.

This brings us to a key point in social constructionism: We co-create each other. The acts we perform as members of an organization not only affect our own and others' work situation; they are involved in shaping our own and others' self-conception and identity. When a manager or a staff member takes up a new job, the relational networks that he or she enters into and the communication in these networks will have a crucial impact on whether the person appears as a competent and dedicated person.

The idea that we co-create each other necessitates a caveat: *for better and for worse*. This point illustrates the close link between social constructionism and relational ethics. In practice it implies a strong obligation for all the members of an organization to consider and pay attention to the effects of their actions on the unfolding interaction patterns and their ability to co-create contexts where all the members of the organization can appear and be recognized as competent and responsible actors in the organization.

5. Ethics and Morality are Embedded in Language, Discourses and Narratives

Some of the stories that are told in organizations are fleeting and vanish in the mist of the past. Others are retold for a long time and become a part of the organization's common understanding in the sense that many actors are able to tell the same story with the same point. One example might be the story about "The time when management forced through a restructuring but failed." How come staff members retell such a story for years with unwavering passion? One answer might be that they do it in the hope that one day the moral message of the story might be heard and acknowledged by management. The moral of the story might be that management fares badly when it fails to listen to the staff or, in the form of a moral message: Management should involve the staff's points of view before restructuring – management should understand that this is only right and proper.

Thus, a narrative or story deals both with the way reality "*is*" and with how it *"ought to be"*. Communities of practice in organizations are held together by more or less compatible versions of reality and a shared morality.

As managers, consultants and employees we have choices as to which of the stories that are told in our organization we want to take part. Which stories do we want to listen to? Which stories do we ask exploratory questions to? Which stories do we help perpetuate? Which new stories do we co-author and co-narrate?

In a social constructionist light, for example, consultants should be wary of allowing lengthy and recurring retellings of stories that are saturated with problems and conflict and in which certain actors are attributed negative personality traits or sinister intentions. Simply by lending an ear to these stories, consultants may cement negative images of self and others. The same challenge faces the manager if a staff member wants to discuss an incident in which a coworker insulted a customer or mishandled a task. It may be tempting to show understanding for the staff member's points of view, but the longer the manager listens, the more entrenched is the negative image of the colleague, and the harder it is for the manager to keep an open mind toward the coworker's version at a later time. In this sense, listening is never "free". Both the stories we tell and the stories we listen to are involved in creating the social world of which we are a part.

6. Power means the Opportunity to Determine the "Truth" and Define the Scope of Possible Actions

In the epistemology of realism, power is seen as something a person possesses in the form of personality traits, motives or resources such as organizational position and formal authority. By contrast, power in a social constructionist perspective is seen as the opportunity to define reality and determine what constitutes "true" knowledge. These opportunities are not evenly distributed – neither in societal debates nor in the ongoing discourses and narratives in organizations.

Many social constructionist writers are inspired by the French philosopher Michel Foucault, who wrote a number of important books from the 1970s until 1984, when he passed away. Foucault undertook extensive historical studies of power forms in Western culture to examine how the individual has been shaped as an object throughout history. How, in the course of history, have people come to be labeled as normal or abnormal, healthy or insane, law-abiding or criminal? Foucault describes both how the scientific development in the human sciences has promoted diagnostics, and how society is organized to marginalize, lock up and exclude the "abnormal", the "insane" and the "criminal" from the public debate. Knowledge and power are inextricably linked. The uneven distribution of power in society reflects differences in the opportunity to produce knowledge which we use to define reality and each other (Dreyfuss & Rabinow, 1983).

Knowledge and power are shaped in the prevailing discourses that determine what it is possible and acceptable to do. *"What it is possible for one person to do to another, under what rights and obligations, is given by the version of events currently taken as 'knowledge' – Therefore the power to act in particular ways, to claim resources, to control or be controlled depends upon the 'knowledges' currently prevailing in a society. We can exercise power by drawing upon discourses which allow our actions to be represented in an acceptable light. Foucault therefore sees power not as some form of possession, which some people have or others do not, but as an effect of discourse. To define the world or a person in a way that allows you to do the things you want is to exercise power"* (Burr, 1995, p. 64). The prevailing narratives in a culture not only overshadow any alternative versions of reality but are also so thoroughly embedded in the mindset of the culture that they come to be taken for granted. They are internalized by the members of the culture, who come to see the mindset as representative of naturally established truths.

Both Foucault and Bruner dealt with conditions on the level of society in Western cultures. In Chapter 7 we discuss how Foucault's ideas about power and knowledge can be unfolded in an organizational setting. In particular, we take a closer look at how the uneven distribution of the power to cast or position oneself and others in the stories that are told affects the characteristics that are attached to managers and employees as well as organizational members' opportunities and restrictions.

7. Appreciative Inquiry is a Path to New Realizations about a Desirable Future

Appreciative Inquiry is in use around the world as an approach to development processes in organizations, societies and international settings. The ideas in Appreciative Inquiry were first published in the journal article *Appreciative Inquiry in Organizational Life* (Cooperrider & Srivasta, 1987) and later in an anthology (Cooperrider & Srivasta, 1999). This first seminal article would become a classic. As mentioned earlier, Cooperrider and Srivasta build on Kenneth J. Gergen's first works on social constructionism. The authors add a small but crucial normative twist to the basic idea of social constructionism: Since we create reality through our choice of focus and the topics we talk about, then let us concentrate on learning about the thoughts, actions, events and interaction patterns that help us move toward a desirable future.

In the article *Positive Image, Positive Action: The Affirmative Basis of Organizing*, which also became a classic, Cooperrider writes, *"Appreciation not only draws our eye toward life, but stirs our feelings, excites our curiosity, and provides inspiration to the envisioning mind. In this sense, the ultimate generative power for the construction of new values and images is the apprehension of that which has value"* (Cooperrider, 1999, p. 122).

This means that an appreciative inquiry into events in organizations should focus on noticing, describing and understanding all those small or large facets of thoughts and actions that generate life and energy, and which bring out managers' and employees' competencies and dedication. Simply noticing things that work well can be challenging enough, given that in the Western culture, we are brought up to notice errors, shortcomings, inadequacies and problems. However, in any organization there is something that works. So why try so hard to study flaws and shortcomings instead of studying what is successful and brings us closer to a desirable future? – to sum up Cooperrider's simple rationale. Thus, the first condition for achieving new insights about what works is to be able to notice something that is of value.

In an interesting note to the article *Appreciative Inquiry in Organizational Life* the authors refer to the physicist Jeremy Hayward, who is quoted as saying, *"I'll see it when I believe it"* and, conversely, *"I won't see it because I don't believe it"*. These statements are accompanied by the following explanation: *"The point is that all observation is filtered through belief systems which act as our personal theories of the world. Thus, what counts as 'fact' depends largely on beliefs associated with theory and therefore on the community of scientists espousing this belief system"* (Cooperrider & Srivasta, 1999, p. 438).

The ability to see reality through an appreciative eye can be enhanced: *"Through both formal and informal learning processes, organizations, like individuals, can develop their metacognitive competence – the capacity to rise above the present and assess their own imaginative processes as they are operating. This enhances their ability to distinguish between affirmative and negative ways of construing the world"* (Cooperrider, 1999, p. 118). As an example of this, Cooperrider mentions that organizational studies that focus on a careful selection of useful experiences, and which offer positive feedback are more likely to contribute to positive organizational development than studies that focus on problems and shortcomings.

Thus, the first and most crucial idea in Appreciative Inquiry has to do with the importance of generating learning processes about the things that work, about what we want in the future, and about the experiences that can bring us closer to the desirable future.

The second idea deals specifically with the importance of generating concrete visions about a desirable future. For this, we need imagination and creativity that exceed the potentials of a problem analysis. In a problem analysis the goal is to narrow in on a few key causes and come up with ways of removing or modifying these causes. The generation of visions for the future opens a far broader field of opportunities. Thus, problem analyses fix our gaze on the past, while Appreciative Inquiry opens up to visions for the future. The rationale is that managers' and employees' actions here and now are shaped far more by their images of the future than by their thoughts about causes in the past. The tricky bit, however, is that our visions of a desirable future are more vague and less concrete than our problem analyses. We simply have a richer language for discussing errors, shortcomings and problems. Typically, for example, it is easier for the staff to describe why they find their manager incompetent than to explain what they consider competent management and how they might invite their manager into a competent interaction. Food for thought.

The capacity of Appreciative Inquiry to help managers and employees to co-create a better future should not be understood in an instrumental sense. In a technical-rational strategy for change, positive projections are used to plan the future based on a desire to achieve certainty and control events. By contrast, the appreciative approach seeks to expand the scope of opportunity by directing attention toward the fleeting and less obvious aspects of life in an organization. In Appreciative Inquiry it is more important to be open to wonder than to be open to change.

The third idea in Appreciative Inquiry expands on the social constructionist idea that we shape our mutual relationships through the language we use. If we choose the individualizing common-sense language that is designed to describe, diagnose and evaluate individual members of the organization we create a distance between the one who is doing the describing and evaluating and the person who is being described and evaluated. Furthermore, labeling someone locks that person into categories that he or she may find irrelevant or inappropriate. Negative labels can be costly for a manager's or a staff member's self-esteem, reputation and opportunities for action in the organization. On the other hand, we can choose an appreciative language that focuses on the relationships and the interdependency of the members of an organization.

If we accept the assumption that we co-create each other, our choice of language and language use becomes a moral choice.

REFLECTIONS

A social constructionist perspective on events in organizations enhances our awareness of the fact that everything we say and do affects relationships, our mutual relatedness and the social world that becomes our reality. Thus, social constructionism entails ethics that makes relationships the center of reflections. We call this relational ethics.

Relational ethics is radically different from our everyday common-sense concept of morality, where the point is to place blame and responsibility with an individual and hold this person accountable for his or her actions and sins of omission. Within the framework of social constructionism, we look instead at how we co-construct meaning and how we share responsibility for the events that unfold.

Realism, with its assumption of a pre-existing and demonstrably objective reality, invites us to define and promote our *rights* in the world that we are exposed to. Social constructionism instead encourages us to try to discover and practice moral *obligations* in a world that we are not only exposed to but actively involved in affirming, strengthening or changing. How to practice the moral obligations based on relational ethics in an organizational setting is the topic of the remainder of this book.

CHAPTER 3

CONTEXT AND SOCIAL RESPONSIBILITY

In Chapter 2 we reviewed the key ideas in social constructionism, which forms the conceptual framework of this book. The notion that what we perceive as reality is construed through language and communication with others is an abstract notion indeed. Nikolas Rose, professor of sociology, writes in the preface to his book *Governing the Soul: The Shaping of the Private Self* (1999) that the notion that scientific findings are socially constructed has come to be commonplace, and that the interesting point now is *how* this construction takes place. We agree with the second part of his claim but not with the first. It is far from trivial to note that what we take to be reality is socially constructed. It is, however, an important point that we need to expand our understanding of the very concrete ways in which language constructs the social reality we participate in. As we wrote in the previous chapter, this premise obligates us to pay attention to relational ethics. We will now take a closer look at the link between philosophy of language and ethics.

Our first step will be to unfold an approach to language that is completely different from our common-sense understanding and traditional scientific schools within the frameworks of realism, objectivism and positivism. In these frameworks language is considered an important tool for describing reality. That understanding is based on the notion that reality exists "out there", open to more or less adequate or correct description by means of language. Social constructionism rests on a very different view of the importance and function of language. Here, the emphasis is instead on the creative powers of language. The philosophers Ludwig Wittgenstein and John Austin played crucial roles in shaping this understanding.

Our next step is to attempt to illuminate the complexity of human interactions and communication. The key concept here is *context*. If language does not derive its meaning from its match with objective reality, then what is the source of the meaning of words? The answer is through *context*. In recent years, the term context has taken on increasing popularity, but it is often applied in a matter-of-fact sense, referring to a frame that unambiguously "is", and which defines what is inside and what is outside the frame – or it is simply used synonymously with the surroundings. Thus, people speak of the organization's context, referring to the stakeholders, the market, the political system, etc., that is, as synonymous with "the situation".

From a social constructionist perspective the term context does not refer to the surrounding of a phenomenon but instead to the active interweaving of *strands of meaning* into a coherent pattern that is related to particular individuals' experiences and actions in concrete situations (Cronen, 1995). *Context* refers to the etymological Latin root: "contexere", which means to weave together. Thus, context is the meaning-constructing pattern in which events unfold. This pattern is not something that "is" just there but something that "happens" through language. Context provides the answer to the question, "What are we doing here and now?" or "What is the meaning of what is going on?" Our language use shapes the context. The words we choose to use and the way in which we interact, help answer the question of what we are doing right now. Only when we feel that we know what we are doing does the single word or utterance become meaningful. Later in this chapter we offer some concrete examples and stories to illustrate the usefulness of the concept of context.

The closing part of this chapter looks at links between language and moral obligations. When we communicate we are not exchanging neutral descriptions of an external or internal reality. From a social constructionist perspective, language has an embedded moral logic. Any "description" springs from cultural, organizational and individual forms of understanding that contain implicit messages about how things "ought to be" and what is considered good or bad, right or wrong. For instance, when employees describe their manager as being visible or invisible, trustworthy or untrustworthy, these statements are not descriptions of a concrete reality but implicit messages about how the manager ought to be.

This understanding of language and context puts social responsibility on the agenda. The words we use make a difference. It is a moral challenge to pay attention to the effects of language and to avoid the words and phrases that do not aid us in constructing a better social world. If a manager wants to understand a staff member who is behaving "oddly", the challenge in a social constructionist perspective is not to examine the person's inner life and interpret his or her intentions, motivations, attitudes, feelings, etc. but rather to pay attention to the possible moral messages of the communication that the staff member participates in. The next step is to rephrase, expand and alter one's own language in order to create new possibilities of moving forward together.

Before we turn to the linguistic philosophers, let us examine an everyday incident that takes place in many different versions when staff members from different organizations are brought together in a staff meeting.

Karen, an internal consultant in a municipality, talks about the merger that her organization recently underwent as four municipalities merged into one:

STORY 1: THE OPEN INVITATION THAT LET AN EMPLOYEE EMBARRASS HERSELF

If you had asked me how things are going two weeks ago, I would have said that everything was fine. But now we've just had this rather unpleasant experience. Last Friday, the staff members of the new HR department were going to meet each other for the first time. It was an exciting day that I had really been looking forward to – we finally knew who the head of department was going to be, and who would be joining the new HR department. The HR manager, Beatrice, had scheduled a morning meeting for all us, which would be concluded with a together lunch.

We were a mixed lot: Employees from the HR departments of the four municipalities plus one person who had been transferred from another department as well as a new employee. Many of us didn't know each other. Beatrice had been head of HR in the second-largest municipality. I thought that she was a good choice. My own HR manager had opted for retirement, so she was not a candidate. I had met Beatrice a couple of times, and I had an excellent impression of her: She seemed experienced, competent, forthcoming and friendly.

Beatrice opened with a very warm welcome. She talked about how much she was looking forward to finally bringing the department together and getting started. She talked about her values and the importance of good working relations and said that it was very important for us to get to know each other well. Therefore she suggested that we start by saying a little bit about ourselves: our job experience, family, hobbies, etc. The first person said that she had been with the municipality for five years, and that she was married, had two kids, etc. The next person said that she was married and expecting her second child. Then it was my turn. I talked a little bit about my job and then said that I had been married for seven years but that we were now getting a divorce, which was difficult, mostly because we didn't agree about where the kids should live. At this point my voice began to shake, and I quickly gave the floor to the next person. The rest of the meeting went by in a fog.

Afterwards, I had been thinking about what happened. I thought it was pretty embarrassing that I wasn't able to talk soberly about my divorce. Sometimes, when I recall the events, I get angry; I don't see why it's any of my coworkers' business. Maybe I would have told them about my divorce at some point, once everything is sorted out, and I could pick who to discuss it with. But in this situation I didn't feel that I had a choice – and then in front of everybody at once! This has reduced my trust in my new boss – not that I discussed it with her. I don't think I can, either; I'm sure she did it with the best intentions. But how do I move on from here in relation to my colleagues? Now they're probably thinking of me as "the one who's getting divorced, and who is going through a rough time."

What is going on here? Apparently, a very well-intentioned manager wanted to get her staff members and the new department off to the best possible start in the new organization. She probably felt that the meeting went well, and that it was nice that the staff members were able to speak openly and honestly about their lives. The other staff members might have felt the same way – we do not know. However, our narrator does not feel that way. She is worried that she might be seen as "the one who's getting divorced, and who is going through a rough time" instead of being seen as an experienced coworker. The combination of the manager's very open invitation and the first colleagues' responses made it difficult for Karen to draw a line between information that is relevant to the job situation versus private information. How can we understand this situation? We will get back to that question later once we have taken a closer look at the creative powers of language and the concept of context.

THE CREATIVE POWERS OF LANGUAGE

The philosopher Ludwig Wittgenstein (1889-1951) wanted to find a new approach to everyday language. In his book *Philosophical Investigations* (1953) Wittgenstein criticized an assumption central to all earlier philosophy. He called this assumption the *name theory*. Name theory implies that language consists of words that are "names" that derive their meaning from the objects they refer to. Wittgenstein claimed that the name theory misleads us into believing in the existence of phenomena to which they seem to refer - such as numbers, values, past, power, causes, happiness, etc. Wittgenstein argued, instead, that words derive their meaning from *use*. A word does not have any inherent meaning that can be defined unambiguously; instead, words derive meaning through the language activities that take place among people. Words also change meaning historically – sometimes they even take on the opposite of the original meaning. In Danish, for example, "sick" can be used as a positive term in teenage slang.

The performance of language activities not only requires knowledge of words and sentence structures but also of the rules that are embedded in the language activity. Here Wittgenstein introduced the metaphor "language games". Just as one must know the rules of chess in order to play, participants in language activities must be aware of the culturally generated rules that apply to the given activity. Thus, language is not separate from reality but produces our everyday life. We are linked together through the language activities in which we engage. This knowledge of language activities is not something we are born with; it is cultural knowledge and acquired through play, mimicry, practice, and real-life experimentation. There is an endless number of language activities which we master more or less skillfully. For example, some organizational members may be excellent negotiators yet still have difficulty practicing small talk in informal situations.

This view of language has important implications for what it means *to understand*. Wittgenstein raised this question but pointed out that the term is misleading. It tempts us to apply the name theory and define *understanding* as an inner phenomenon in an individual. According to Wittgenstein, the statement "Now I understand!" should not be understood as a report or a claim of any inner or outer phenomenon but rather as a signal that it is now possible to move on, for example in relation to solving a problem. *"Think of the tools in a tool-box: there is a hammer, pliers, a saw, a screw-driver, a rule, a glue-pot, glue, nails and screws. — The functions of words are as diverse as the functions of these objects"* (Wittgenstein, 1953, p. 6). Not only do words have different functions; they also serve as tools that may help or hinder our progress, depending how elegantly we apply them.

Wittgenstein also used the term *bewitchment*. Words may bewitch us and fixate us, preventing us from moving forward. This line of thinking leads to two key points. The first point is that when people speak about the past, they are not engaged in providing adequate and correct descriptions of past events. Rather, they are engaged in a language activity that may involve confessing a past wrong, accusing someone of something, or telling a story where all obstacles were overcome. Understanding is what results when stories produce an insight into how we can proceed. Stories about the past are interesting because of their capacity to shed light on the future.

The other key point is that when language is not seen as a tool for describing reality but as part of a language activity that shapes human inter-actions, helping or hindering our progress, then all change and development must begin in language. That is a revolutionizing thought in relation to the methods that are commonly applied in organizations to promote change and development. We will revisit this important point in the following chapters.

Words at Work

John Langshaw Austin (1911-1960) was a philosopher of language and ethics who developed many ideas related to Wittgenstein's. Austin viewed language as action and was interested in its social function. According to Austin, language has a performative power, it *does something* to our relationships at the same time as it describes. His path to this important idea went through careful studies of everyday language and its speech acts, especially with regard to verbs. In a study of the creative powers of language Austin was particularly interested in verbs, the doing-words. In his much-quoted book *How to do things with words* (1962), Austin estimated that there were thousands of doing-words in English. These words are filled with meaning and conventions. The same utterance can take on different performative power. The sentence *"Try, and see what happens"* can be, for example, an order, a permission, a request, a demand, a plea, a suggestion, a recommendation, or a warning. To understand an utterance we must know something about the circumstances in which the utterance is made.

Many verbs are performatives, which are characterized by two key features: Firstly, they are not descriptive or statements of fact. Secondly, they are part of actions that go beyond merely saying something. Austin has several amusing examples of this. For example the verb "christen". When the word "christen" is uttered, something happens. The ship or the child gets a name. The statement "I christen this ship the Queen Elizabeth" uttered while a bottle is smashed against the side of the ship cannot be assessed as true or false. The statement and the act are inextricably linked. Austin speaks of a performative sentence or simply "a performative". A performative must be assessed on a different set of criteria than true or false: It must be assessed on whether it was successful or not: *"Besides the uttering of the words of the so called performative, a good many other things have as a general rule to be right and go right if we are to be said to have happily brought off our action. What these are we may hope to discover by looking at and classifying types of case in which something goes wrong and the act – marrying, betting, bequeathing, christening, or what not – is therefore at least to some extent a failure: the utterance is then, we may say, not indeed false but in general unhappy. And for this reason we will call the doctrine of the things that can be and go wrong on the occasion of such utterances, the doctrine of the Infelicities"* (Austin, 1962, p. 14). His analysis leads to a set of conditions that must be met for the speech act to be considered successful. These conditions are listed below in a slightly edited, simplified version:

1. In society there must exist a conventional procedure that is generally accepted. In the example mentioned above, there must be rules specifying what rituals are required in christening a ship and who should be in charge of the rituals.

2. The person who performs the speech act must be entitled or authorized to do so. Not just anyone can perform the act of christening. If an unauthorized person performs the christening the speech act is unsuccessful in the sense that it is not valid.

3. The specific situation must adhere to the conventional procedure. Here, Austin mentions an example where a person who is already married enters into marriage and performs the speech act "I do" in response to the pastor's question. This situation does not adhere to the conventional rules.

4. The procedure must be followed correctly and in full.

5. If the conventional rule set prescribes that the involved parties have to think and feel in a particular way when they perform the speech act, they must do so. The speech act "I do" presupposes that the speaker actually wants to enter into marriage. Otherwise, the marriage act is formally valid but less effective.

6. If the conventional procedure requires the involved parties to act in a particular way, they must do so. For example, the speech act

"to promise" requires the person to subsequently do as promised. Otherwise the speech act is unsuccessful in the sense that it is performed but "hollow".

To illustrate these points, Austin continues to explore the example with the ship that was to be christened the Queen Elizabeth. He asks the audience at his lecture to imagine that he were present at the christening as a guest and then grabbed the champagne bottle and said "I christen this ship the Mr. Stalin." Scandalous! The speech act would clearly be unsuccessful. Not only would the ship not in fact be christened the Mr. Stalin, but Austin would have made a terrible fool of himself because he was unauthorized. For the procedure to be performed correctly and in full the person must be authorized to perform the act.

Why is Austin's analysis interesting? As we see it, it offers a completely different approach to understanding language and communication. To succeed with our speech acts these six conditions must be met. That makes communication and understanding a complicated affair with a big emphasis on practical wisdom, that is, knowledge of how events are performed correctly in certain cultural and social contexts.

Let us apply Wittgenstein's and Austin's ideas in relation to Story 1: *The Open Invitation that let an Employee embarrass Herself*. For example, how can we understand the manager's introduction? Was that a successful speech act? To answer this question we turn to Austin's criteria for a successful speech act.

A round of introduction in an organization can be understood as a language activity that we can perform to the extent that we have learned how. It may seem a rather simple and trivial event not needing any considerations.

But on closer inspection, we find that the opening to an introduction round is based on extensive – culturally generated – conventional knowledge about norms for what the participants should and should not do. By "conventional" we mean knowledge that we take for granted as members of the Western culture. This language activity involves norms about taking turns, about how long each participant speaks (not too long, not too briefly) and about how the participants should respond to someone else's self-introduction (preferably no comments and definitely no corrections). There is a powerful norm that everyone should participate. In the situation outlined in Story 1, it would be a clear violation of the norms if someone had said, "I don't wish to speak," or "I'll pass." Not to mention if someone had said, "I would rather make a phone call to X" and left the room. Once an introduction round has started all the participants have to help complete it.

Similarly, there are common cultural norms as to what the participants in an introduction round bring up. Some topics are clearly within the norms, including previous workplaces, current work tasks and ongoing education activities, while some things are clearly off-topic, such as bodily functions. Thus, it would be highly unconventional in an introduction round to mention one's currently excellent digestion or elevated blood pressure. In the space between these culturally defined categories is a huge grey area where conventional norms make no particular prescriptions. That may include topics that are typically included in a C.V.: marital status, spouse's name, number of children, hobbies, membership of associations, etc. If this were a job interview, the participants would have access to written information about this from the applicant's C.V., and thus many would find it legitimate to include it in a job interview. Others would not. From our experience with recruiting and career counseling we know that women often hesitate to provide information about their family situation in their C.V. because they are worried that the topic might become too prominent in a job interview. An interesting Danish Ph.D. dissertation by M.A. Jann Scheuer (1998) about language and communication in job interviews documents that this concern is not unfounded. One finding from a study of job interviews in three companies was that female applicants were interviewed more extensively about their children and daycare arrangements than male applicants. Consequently, male job seekers had more time to talk about their qualifications and job experience than female job candidates did. Thus, a candidate's presentation of him/herself in a job interview is a grey area governed by ambiguous conventional knowledge about what topics are legitimate to introduce, and how.

This ambiguity in the understanding of legitimate topics in a round of introductions in an organization has to do with the different traditions embedded in our culture as to how we should understand and know an individual. In the framework of the prevailing individualist perspective and the discourse on the necessity of personal growth, the manager's invitation to a presentation of *the whole person* and *the whole life* makes sense. In extension of the social constructionist ideas that we discussed in Chapter 2, a clearer definition of legitimate topics as job-related aspects (such as experience, job tasks, particular fields of interest in relation to work, etc.) might have given Karen and the other participants a better basis for presenting themselves as competent professionals.

How do these considerations effect an assessment of the successfulness of the open invitation to the round of introductions? In relation to Austin's characteristics rounds of introductions are based on conventional knowledge and well-known ground rules, but these rules are *ambiguous* and open to interpretation. Thus, the participants in Story 1 are not on safe ground relying on conventional knowledge. From Karen's story, we do not know how much the manager had thought about the situation. The manager's introduction to the meeting suggests that she had given a great deal of thought to how she wanted to appear as a leader, but it is far from certain that she had considered the consequences that her precise choice of words might have on the staff members' ability to present themselves as competent professionals. Karen might have appeared to the others as "the one who's getting divorced, and who is going through a rough time." She would probably prefer being seen as "the one with the interesting job experience about ..." or as "the one from the Municipality of X". The social power of language is a force to be reckoned with. Karen found that the way she introduced herself made it hard for her to see a way to proceed in her relationship with her new colleagues.

According to Wittgenstein's ideas, this situation did not improve mutual understanding as far as Karen was concerned: It became *more* difficult for her to move on. Karen faced the task of repairing the image she might have projected to her coworkers. Karen's story does not reveal what she would do from then on. It is our guess that she is going to spend some time thinking about how to make her comeback and create a situation that lets her introduce herself anew. We also guess that she is going to try hard to shut down the topic of her divorce. We do not know how Karen's coworkers experienced the round of introduction. It is also difficult to predict how they might respond to a possible attempt by Karen at a comeback.

Karen's story is an initial illustration of the role of language in creating our social reality. However, we need some additional concepts for a better grasp of the process.

INTERACTION AS THE COORDINATION OF MEANING

The theory of Coordinated Management of Meaning (CMM) is very help-ful for understanding the complexity of the micro-social processes in every-day life. The first ideas and models in the CMM theory were developed more than 30 years ago, initially in an article by W. Barnett Pearce (1976) and later in a book by W. Barnett Pearce and Vernon Cronen: *Communication, action and meaning* (1980). In the following decades these ideas were developed further, both by the original authors and by a far-flung and steadily growing circle of researchers, theorists and practitioners in consultation, therapy, education, counseling, management and organization development. To mark the 30th anniversary of the CMM theory, the journal *Human Systems* put out a special issue with research contributions from authors in ten countries and on four continents (Pearce & Kearney (eds.) 2004).

In 2005, the Danish psychological publisher Dansk psykologisk Forlag invited W. Barnett Pearce to write an updated version of his important book *Interpersonal Communication: Making Social Worlds* (Pearce, 1994). Pearce accepted the invitation and wrote a new manuscript that was translated into Danish and published to a Danish audience. The book, which had the Danish title *Kommunikation og skabelsen af sociale verdener* (Pearce, 2007a), was later on published in English as *Making Social Worlds: A Communication Perspective* (Pearce, 2007b).

From the outset, Pearce and Cronen chose to call their theory the theory of the *Coordinated Management of Meaning*. The idea for the name came from a situation where they observed two mechanics who were working on a motorcycle; in this process the two mechanics were able to coordinate their actions in a manner that to the outside observers seemed highly intricate –

without speaking. How did they manage this feat? How did they achieve this level of coordination? The use of the term *management* was inspired by this situation and thus originally referred to managing or handling something – not to the notion of control. According to the theory, no individual is able to control the coordination of acts or the construction of meaning with a particular direction or any particular content; instead, meaning and coordination is achieved in an interaction between the individuals who are involved in the events. Thus, we have decided to leave out the term management altogether and refer instead to the *coordination of action and meaning*.

In his book Pearce argues for the importance of applying a communication perspective to all the events we are involved in: *"If you look carefully, you can see an implicit theory of communication in everything that people say or do with each other. That theory matters. It prefigures the content and quality of the conversations people have with each other and these conversations have afterlives. As the afterlives from many such conversations extend and intertwine, they comprise the social worlds in which the people involved in those conversations – and you and I – live"* (Pearce, 2007b, p. 30). An important point in this quote is that conversations have an afterlife. The key issue in a conversation is not what we describe or understand but the questions, "What are we doing here?", "What is going on here and now?" and "How do we move on from here?" The answers to these questions cannot be neutral but contain a moral dimension – an implicit understanding of what we *should* do now and in the future.

In his 2007 book, Pearce unfolds an alternative to the traditional understanding of communication, according to which it is possible to transfer information about reality from one person to another: *"Using the term 'coordination' as a way of understanding ... is part of the paradigm that I called in chapter 2 the 'social construction' approach to communication. It suggests that, instead of a correspondence between mental state and action, we pose questions and look for answers in the flow of actions themselves. That is, we understand what people say and do as taking 'turns' in patterns of communication, not as 'signs' pointing to something else"* (Pearce, 2007b, pp. 88-89). In practice this means that if we see a manager or a staff member do something odd, we will attempt to understand the pattern of communication that makes the action meaningful – instead of trying to look inside the person to put our finger on what is wrong with him or her.

Our implicit choice of communication theory affects what we are interested in, what we look for, and what it takes for us to feel that we understand. In the traditional understanding of communication, which is associated with individual-focused psychology, it is assumed that information is transferred between minds. It is also assumed that actions can be viewed as indicative of inner states (motives, emotions, intentions, needs, etc.), and that true understanding is predicated on the ability to identify links between actions and inner states. If such links cannot be determined, according to this understanding one has only achieved "superficial" knowledge. Thus, the key is to look for explanations inside the individual. Mutual understanding, from this traditional point of view, consists in an exchange of recognizable descriptions of inner states between two autonomous individuals where the recipient understands the sender's message as it was intended by the sender. This perspective also implies a belief that greater knowledge about links between actions and inner phenomena will lead to better mutual understanding, greater predictability and an enhanced potential for controlling one's own and others' actions. So, what happens if the transfer of information is unsuccessful in the sense that the recipient gets a completely different message than the one the sender intended? How will a sender handle this situation?

The traditional understanding of communication defines three obvious possibilities: First, the sender may conclude that the message was not clear enough and therefore try to make it more specific and then repeat it. Let us imagine a manager who sends an e-mail to his or her staff asking for suggestions for the agenda for the next department meeting. No suggestions emerge. The manager may now choose to send a new e-mail with more specific instructions and a definite deadline. Still no response. At this point, the manager might conclude that there could be something wrong with the transmission itself. Perhaps the e-mail did not get through? Hence, she walks through the building to tell each staff member that suggestions are more than welcome. Still, no suggestions. Now she might very well begin to wonder what is wrong with the staff. Are they dim? Do they lack motivation? Or do they not like their boss? The manager begins to interpret the staff members' inner states.

Here there is a very interesting link between traditional clinical psychology with its focus on the individual and the traditional perception of communication as transmission. Both rely on implicit moral requirements. The manager ought to clarify his or her intentions with the message, be honest and sincere and express his or her feelings. Similarly, the staff members should clarify their reasons for not offering suggestions. What are they up to? Why are they acting this way? The staff members should express how they perceive their manager: What does the act of calling for suggestions signify to them? A demanding boss? A democratic manager? The assumption is that if all these points are laid on the table the parties will be able to understand each other and move on. Let us imagine a department meeting where the manager brings up this series of events within this framework of understanding. For example, the manager might ask, "Why haven't you provided any suggestions? Don't you care about this meeting? Don't you realize how frustrating it is for me as head of the department to receive nothing from you? Don't you read your e-mails, or did you not understand what I wrote? Please, tell me your honest opinion." The prognosis for such a meeting is probably rather poor. Let us therefore examine an alternative approach.

Here, we can find inspiration in Pearce's perspective of communication: *"In the social construction model, communication is more a way of making the social world rather than talking about it, and this is always done with other people. Rather than 'What did you mean by that?' the relevant questions are 'What are we making together?' 'How are we making it?' and 'How can we make better social worlds?'"* (Pearce, 2007b, pp. 30-31). Within this approach, the manager might instead initiate a dialogue with questions such as, *"How can we plan and carry out a good meeting together?"*, *"How would you as staff members like to influence the agenda?"* and *"What ideas do you have for the process of determining the agenda?"*

In this perspective, it is not enough to use *spectator knowledge*. We also need to include *participatory knowledge*. This excellent distinction is presented by Pearce (2007b). Spectator knowledge is the knowledge we acquire when we observe phenomena and events from the outside. Positivist research aims to produce knowledge that is independent of the observer and the observer's methods, and which can lead to universal laws. The bulk of the curriculum in schools and institutions of higher learning deals with spectator knowledge. Thorough and reliable spectator knowledge is a key condition for taking exams and moving through the education system. However, Pearce explains vividly how he finally discovered that spectator knowledge could not help him determine what to do in real-life situations: *"The kind of knowledge that we need to participate in a process is very different from that which we need as observers. Specifically, spectator knowledge is summarized in propositions; participatory knowledge is expressed in wise actions. The propositions of spectator knowledge have an affinity for the verb 'to be': participatory knowledge has an affinity for words describing oughtness ... If we try to use spectator knowledge to describe our experience within social worlds, we wind up describing ourselves as alienated or victims; in the language of participatory knowledge, we can at least sometimes act wisely and effectively"* (Pearce, 2007b, pp. 52-53).

Over the years, Pearce has done extensive research into interpersonal communication. Based on this research he states that mutual understanding is not necessary for communication to take place. People have no problem coordinating their actions and moving on in meetings, conversations and wordless work situations even if they do not agree about the meanings of the individual actions and do not know what the other person is thinking. How is this possible? Here, we need a new set of concepts to help us explore the micro-social processes in the communication patterns that occur in organizations and in the continuous flow of actions.

Speech Acts

For Pearce, a "speech act" is the smallest unit of meaning in the ongoing flow of actions. To us there is a kinship in ideas between the CMM theory and Austin's thoughts on the performative power of language, the diversity of speech acts and the normative basis of the successful performance of speech acts.

A speech act is not just a line or an utterance but a sequence of lines that are exchanged between at least two persons: *"I don't think there are, or can be, any single-turn speech acts; they are co-constructed in a sequence of interactive "turns". The ideal or prototypical structure of a speech act is a three-turn sequence or "conversational triplet"* (Pearce, 2007b, p. 117). The individuals engaging in a speech act cannot individually determine its meaning. A single utterance can develop into several speech acts depending on the context and the subsequent lines. A speech act shapes our social reality. For example, it may constitute a promise, a reprimand, an order, an insult, an offense, an invitation, a compliment, a threat, a warning, a declaration of trust, a joke, a rejection, etc. A word or an utterance does not have any particular meaning in itself but depends on what happened before and what follows. Here, the CMM theory latches on to Wittgenstein's idea that the meaning of language is constructed through language use in a particular context. Here, we will play a little with Pearce's example of a single utterance that has the potential of becoming several different speech acts: *"The door is open"* (Pearce, 2007b, p. 116). Within a technical approach to language and communication this utterance would be understood as a statement describing the position of the door in relation to the door jamb. In a social constructionist perspective of communication the picture is quite different. The utterance does not become meaningful until we know more about the situation. We might imagine that this brief four-word sentence was said by a manager to an employee toward the end of a pay rise negotiation. In that case it might mean, "Okay, we're done now, you can go." The employee might choose to perceive the sentence in this manner and perceive the speech act as an end to the meeting and say, for example, "Fine, I also think that's as far as we'll get today," Here lies a crucial point: The manager's utterance only takes on meaning once the employee has responded.

The employee can also perceive it as a warning not to let others overhear the content of the agreement and then respond, "I'm quite aware of that. I'm speaking very softly." Or the employee may perceive the utterance as a request for him to close the door to keep others from overhearing the conversation. In that case, the employee might get up and close the door without saying a word. Alternatively, the employee may choose to understand the four words as a sign that the manager is reopening the negotiations – or maybe even that the employee has been fired and is asked to leave the workplace.

The statement *"The door is open"* might occur in many other types of situations. In a train compartment it might be a reprimand: "Why don't you shut the door!" In an informal conversation during the lunch break where two colleagues are debating a difficult problem it might mean "My door is always open to you. You can count on my assistance any time." In that situation it is shaped as the speech act of "an invitation or an offer of help" Meaning is shaped depending on the way in which the involved individuals coordinate their actions in a particular situation.

Let us consider the pay rise negotiation in the scenario where the employee gets up and closes the door, expecting the manager to now finally announce a number for the pay rise. Again, there are several possibilities. If the manager says, "Right, you've convinced me. I will give you an additional 500 dollars a month," the speech act "entering into confidential agreement" was realized. But that is not the only possibility. The manager might also say, "You don't have to close the door. The meeting is over." In that case we have yet another opening and as yet undefined possibility for the development in this series of events. In harmonious conversations it is possible to accomplish a speech act in three turns. In less harmonious conversations it may take many turns before the actors are able to coordinate their actions. Let us unfold this possibility further:

1. The manager says, "The door is open."
2. The employee gets up and closes the door.
3. The manager says, "You don't have to close the door. The meeting is over."
4. The employee says, "You can't be serious. Three months ago, you promised me a pay rise."
5. The manager then says, "That may be, but the situation has changed. We'll have to talk again in two months."
6. The employee says, "I guess we will then. But I want you to know that I'm not happy with this."

How do we label the speech act that is shaped in this exchange? It resembles the conclusion of a meeting; however, the employee has reshaped it to be just as close to the speech act of "a broken promise". What is defined as the overall speech act probably depends on whether we ask the employee or the manager.

In relation to the linear mindset of common-sense logic the CMM theory offers a revolutionizing possibility of taking a creative and reflexive stance to the continuous flow of events in everyday life. Common-sense logic relies on chronology in determining chains of cause and effect. It is taken for granted that past events direct current actions, which in turn influence future actions. In a social constructionist perspective it is, however, an important point that the process of constructing meaning is also shaped by subsequent actions and events; this point has considerable implications for our understanding of responsibility and morality.

Another important aspect of speech acts has to do with the moral dimensions of events. In his first presentation of the CMM theory Pearce wrote about the *logical force* of others' actions, but in his latest book he writes that had he been writing the book today he would have preferred the term *moral force* (Pearce, 2007 b, p. 120). In the linear thinking of common-sense logic we are seen as doing something depending on what the other(s) did *first*. Other people's actions can pressure us into *responding in kind* or *sharing our honest, sincere opinion*, such as "This is rubbish," or "You sound like a moron." We may feel that we have to act in a particular way because of what the other person did. Events are shaped into narratives, and embedded in these narratives are habitual rules that we use to interpret not only what happens but also what we are now morally obligated to do (Oliver, 2005). Here Pearce reminds us to pause and to avoid simply following the force of common-sense logic without reflection. In order to discover what we might do instead, we also need to understand the situation that frames the speech act. Here, Pearce uses the term *episode*.

Episodes

According to Pearce, episodes are the second-smallest unit of meaning in interpersonal communication; they consist of a sequence of speech acts. A sequence is limited in time and thus has a beginning and an end. However, not all events take place within the time frame that is being considered. Only the speech acts that are perceived as relevant and as being linked together as a story are included in the episode. In the CMM theory, thus, the term *episode* is used to examine how people impose order on the continuous and more or less chaotic flow of events.

As Pearce states, our social world has an episodic structure where the single moments, actions or events can be seen as parts of several types of episodes. Based on the previous example of the many potential meanings of the sentence *"The door is open"*, it is easy to imagine how the small act of closing or opening a door can fit into several different episodes. The interesting question is, therefore, how people manage to attribute meaning to both the small, unnoticed and the dramatically visible events of everyday life. Which speech acts are co-created, which are selected, and how are they arranged into episodes? That brings us to an important psychological point: People rely on selective perception and selective memory. We are neither able to notice all the details in a situation nor to remember everything we experience. Therefore, we are all engaged in selection processes – perhaps different and conflicting selection processes. Our selection process depends on the particular interpretation we have defined as the *frame of the episode*. Pearce (2007b) describes different ways of framing our interpretation of an episode. Firstly, we *punctuate* events, determining when an episode begins and ends. In the ongoing flow of events that make up everyday life we usually do not notice that we punctuate. We simply feel that we experience events as they are. Nevertheless, punctuation is an active act that has a strong impact on both the attribution of meaning and the coordination of action. A determination of when the conflict, the argument or the cooperation began has a significant impact on the course of the story and the allocation of responsibility and blame: *"My point is that perceptions of beginnings and ends of any episode are matters of responsibility… If we take responsibility for the way we punctuate episodes, we can create opportunities for unusually productive discussions"* (Pearce, 2007b, p. 139). Typically, we punctuate in such a way that "everything" began with someone else's actions. Our own action is seen as a natural reaction to what someone else did. The discovery that others may have made different punctuations can enable actions that do not simply follow the moral force of common-sense logic: "When he insults me, of course I have to stand up for myself." Thus, determining "who started it," and "who got the last word," has a crucial impact on the way in which events are combined into episodes and on the possibilities and difficulties of coordinating subsequent actions. Thus, punctuation and morality are closely related.

Secondly, we frame events that occur within the times of beginning and end as parts of a coherent story. Pearce calls this *emplotment*. The plot in a story is its underlying story line. Let us consider an example that many probably recognize. An organizational member says, "At the latest department meeting there was a lively debate, and everybody was engaged and loud. About halfway into the meeting, many people were talking at the same time. The head of the department was also very active in the debate." Is this the story of an incompetent leader who is unable to manage a department meeting? Or a creative brainstorm? Or a staff group that is ambivalent to management? The "same" events can be fitted into very different story lines. Any series of events can be shaped into many different stories. Within the CMM theory, emplotment is more than a way of describing events. The underlying story line helps shape the actors' social world and is also implicitly involved in forming moral messages. All stories have a moral message.

UNPREDICTABLE AND UNCONTROLLABLE COMMUNICATION IN ORGANIZATIONS

As we saw earlier in this chapter, the question of how to understand a speech act cannot be answered until we know the preceding as well as the *subsequent* acts. In contrast to common-sense logic, where the chronological sequence of events determines our sense of being able to pinpoint causes, chronology is sidelined in the CMM theory. As Pearce puts it, *"First, the turns that are chronologically adjacent aren't necessarily the turns that comprise the triplet. We often engage in complex patterns of coordination, so when we think about how our actions in the present turn will move other actions toward completion, we should be open to the possibility that what we do 'now' will have greatest effect on actions that happened some turns ago, not necessarily the most recent turn"* (Pearce, 2007b, p. 118). This quote illustrates the complexity of everyday events where the actors will make different punctuations depending on their position. Determining when "it" (the conflict, the argument, the collaboration, etc.) began is crucial for the definition of the actors' moral obligations and entitlements.

In organizations, complexity also increases because the ongoing flow of events occurs in many places in the organization and in ways that are impossible for any single person to grasp. That makes it very difficult to use chronology as one's organizing principle. Each actor only sees and hears some of the lines that are part of a complex pattern of actions. We will now examine a flow of events that got out of hand in an organization, where the task of coordinating meanings and utterances became unmanageable. The events play out in an IT company. The main character is the 29-year-old IT-specialist Hank, who has a very special professional profile that is important for the company.

STORY 2: FRIENDLY CONCERN
OR SEXUAL HARASSMENT?

Hank had joined the company four months earlier. He was excited to get the job, especially because in addition to handling tasks in his own department, he was going to work as part of an interdepartmental development team, which allowed him to build on his specialist knowledge. A month after he joined the company the team members had been selected, and the first meeting was scheduled. Then he was unexpectedly called in for a meeting with his supervisor, Helen, who told him that he would not be joining the development team in spite of the previous agreement, as he had been accused of sexual harassment by another member of the team, Diane. Hank could not believe his ears: sexual harassment!? And Diane!?

Helen asked what had happened between them. Hank said that a few weeks after he had started, he had noticed that Diane looked very unhappy. One day he had seen her in the lunch room, wiping a tear from her eye. He had sent her an e-mail, saying something like, "I saw you in the lunch room. You looked so sad. Is there anything I can do for you?" Diane had not responded. Helen asked to see the e-mail. She did – and did not see anything wrong with it.

Helen said that she had been contacted by Diane's supervisor, Karen, who said that Diane had perceived the e-mail as an "improper advance", and that Diane refused to work on the same team as Hank. Karen had made it clear that Diane, who had been with the company for five years, was indispensable for the development task.

Hank did not know what had hit him. It was commonplace to send e-mails to each other during the day. The tone was quite liberal, and he did not think that his e-mail was in any way more offensive than the standard. Perhaps less so, as they could sometimes be quite sassy. He simply wanted to help. He had been raised on strong Christian values and was taught to be helpful to others. It had always been important for him to help others – especially if they were troubled. He barely knew Diane, but she had looked so sad!

Helen suggested that they all meet to discuss what had happened: Karen, Diane, Hank and Helen. Hank agreed, and Helen tried to schedule a date. That proved difficult. Diane refused to be in the same room as Hank. Karen did not want to force her to do it, since she was worried that Diane might quit. She could be quite temperamental.

Hank felt unfairly treated. To think that he, who had always placed such a high price on moral behavior, was accused of sexual harassment; the thought was almost unbearable. He felt it was cowardly of Diane to refuse to even speak with him. If he had written anything negative, he could understand the commotion. But his e-mail had been positive.

Helen assigned a different employee to the development team. She apologized to Hank that she had to make this decision. She also said that she could sympathize if he was angry about being accused of something as outrageous as sexual harassment. It was during this conversation that she offered him to see an external coach, in part to debrief the events and in part to work on his communication skills to keep something similar from happening again.

A few months went by, and Hank was getting bored. His work was too routine and not challenging enough. He had begun thinking about looking for a job somewhere else, when something unexpected happened. A minor restructuring took place that made it natural to move him to another department. He agreed and was fairly pleased with the change. He felt that Helen had backed him up throughout, but he still did not see what he might have done wrong. After all, he was only trying to help.

What is the story here? We might surmise that everybody involved feels that something went terribly wrong. But that is probably where the agreement ends, for what exactly is it that went wrong? If we apply linear, common-sense logic, we will be trying to ascertain where the problem lies, what the core of problem is, what the cause of the problem is, and who is to blame. An investigation along those lines would quickly determine that the parties are experiencing different problems and different causes. To Diane, the problem is that she is exposed to sexual harassment; to Hank that he is not only unjustly accused but also excluded from an assignment that he had been looking forward to. To Helen the problem might be that she has to disappoint a staff member, and that her department lost influence in the development team. To Karen the problem is probably that one of her key employees is at risk of losing interest in staying on.

A problem analysis based on common-sense logic might generate spectator knowledge but not the participatory knowledge that the parties involved might use to create a different social world than the one characterized by "sexual harassment" and the exclusion of Hank from the development team. Let us instead try to apply the ideas outlined above to understand the creation of speech acts and episodes.

How is it that Hank's e-mail is arranged into a speech act that is labeled an *"improper advance"*? As we have seen earlier, singular utterances are meaningless in themselves. It takes at least three lines of interpersonal communication before an utterance can be interpreted as a speech act. That points to the first major complication. The e-mail is not part of an interpersonal communication, which requires direct contact between the parties. E-mail communication is a risky form of communication, as they are issued forth "into the blue" without guiding context markers, such as time, place and relationship. In this case Hank and Diane apparently did not know each other very well, which means that the e-mail was issued in a vaguely defined relationship. The absence of context markers leaves the field wide open to interpretation. It is unlikely that Hank gave this any thought. Perhaps he acted implicitly on the traditional understanding of communication as transmission and expected Diane to understand his e-mail in accordance with his intention of being helpful. Since this proved not to be the case, there was every reason – from Hank's perspective – to be shocked.

Meaning in communication cannot be created by the speaker or writer alone. It takes at least two persons and three lines. Hank's e-mail was a failed speech act because he did not receive any reaction or affirmation. We imagine that the e-mail was arranged as the speech act "an improper advance" during the conversation between Diane and her supervisor, Karen, and that this was also when the episode was labeled *"sexual harassment"*. We do not know exactly what was said. All we know is that when the story reached Helen, it had become a story about *"sexual harassment"*.

How does Diane manage to define the episode as sexual harassment? Here, punctuation is essential. She punctuates the e-mail as the first act. Hank makes the first move. Maybe she does not think that she said or did anything that his e-mail could possibly be a response to. Therefore, it must spring from Hank's character (maybe Diane perceives him as a "creepy fellow"). Here the moral force of common-sense logic comes into play and might make Diane think something like, "Since Hank is the way he is, I will have to protect myself from him and avoid all contact. Ergo, I refuse to be on the same team as him." This punctuation is crucial for the plot. In this plot Diane positions herself as a victim, Hank as the villain, and the supervisor as her rescuer.

How might it all look from Hank's point of view? According to the story, his punctuation is different, as Diane's acting sad is what gets the ball rolling. It is her sad demeanor that makes him write the e-mail. Maybe he also thinks they had some previous contact in the form of a nod and a "hi". We do not know. But it is likely that Hank perceives his e-mail as line number two, and that he expects affirmation of his offer of help. Since that does not happen, and he is unpredictably contacted by Helen, the communication goes haywire, and it becomes extremely difficult for everyone involved to coordinate their actions.

Helen attempts to bring the two together, but she fails. The relationship between Hank and Diane is not reestablished, and the story about sexual harassment is not dismantled.

We do not know how things developed later. Maybe Diane was satisfied that Hank was excluded from the team and then suspended the story about sexual harassment. It is also possible that her moral outrage drives her to tell some of her coworkers what had happened to her – if only with the good intention of warning them about Hank.

Could things have worked out differently? Absolutely. There are many possibilities for achieving a different course. Here we will turn to a very interesting concept from CMM theory: *conversational bifurcation points*. In the series of events outlined above, there were many bifurcation points where a different utterance or a different act than the one that was chosen might have taken events in a very different direction. If we examine the details of the sequence, we can identify various points at which everybody involved might have done something different from what they did.

Hank might have considered whether he should make his offer of help in an e-mail or face to face, and he might have taken some time to imagine how Diane would perceive his contact. Instead of sending an e-mail, he might have stopped by Diane's table in the lunch room next time he saw her and struck up a conversation. Based on Diane's reactions he would then have had a chance to *fine-tune* his communication and adapt creatively to the course of the conversation. As things turned out, he chose e-mail as his medium. What could he have done later in the process? From the time when he was confronted with the allegations of sexual harassment, things got difficult for him. It is clear that he felt that he was treated unjustly by being cast as a villain – a role that was in stark contrast to his identity as a helpful person, but his possibility of escaping this role was limited. If he had attempted to talk to Diane by stopping her in the hallway or in the lunch room, it is likely that she would have interpreted this initiative as yet another improper advance. The term "sexual harassment" risks putting the "villain" check mate, effectively shutting down communication. To establish a direct conversation it would be necessary to have a third party present, for example Helen. Thus, another possibility for him would be to insist with Helen that she set up a meeting between Diane and himself.

When Diane received the e-mail in the first place she might have chosen to check her initial response and instead approach Hank's situation and
the possible message in the e-mail with curiosity. She might have sent an e-
mail back saying, "Thanks for your concern, but you're wrong. I am fine and
don't need any help." She might also have sent him a sharper e-mail that was
closer to her initial interpretation, reading "I think it's best if you just mind
your own business." Whatever wording she had chosen, any response would
have given Hank the opportunity to fine-tune his next line, and contact
could have been maintained. Diane might also have chosen to contact Hank
to ask him what he intended to achieve with his e-mail. Or she might have
accepted Helen's invitation for a meeting including all four of them.
Naturally, she might also have taken Hank at his word and accepted his offer
of help, or she might have shrugged the whole thing off and ignored his e-
mail. Diane had many obvious bifurcation points, and her choice could have
led to a wealth of different scenarios. Whether she considered any of these
bifurcation points and scenarios we do not know.

In her conversation with Diane, Karen might have offered alternative
interpretations of the episode. She might also have insisted on including
other people in interpreting the incident, and as Diane's supervisor she
might have required Diane to show up for the meeting that Helen was
attempting to schedule.

Helen might have held on to the idea of a four-way meeting or, as an
alternative, had a meeting with Diane alone as a first step in arranging the
four-way meeting.

The interesting point here is that everybody involved could have acted
differently at multiple bifurcation points and thus have taken the sequence of

events off the track that led to a story about sexual harassment. The common-sense question, "Who is to blame?" clearly becomes meaningless. Everybody involved has a shared responsibility for the pattern of communication that emerged and for the slightly poorer social world that resulted. We will now take a closer look at how this shared responsibility can be managed.

SOCIAL RESPONSIBILITY

The big question raised by the CMM theory is how we can act in a socially responsible way to improve our ability to master forms of communication that help create a jointly desirable social world. That is no simple task, since actions and events are interwoven in ways that are impossible for any individual to grasp. In Pearce's words, *"I think some episodes develop something like the movements of flocks of birds. They are made when two or more people follow their own rules for action and these actions intermesh in ways not intended by any of the participants, who are often surprised, dismayed, or delighted by the results. This is perhaps the most capricious and unsophisticated way in which episodes can be realized. It 'works' because so many of us draw from the same well of rules for meaning and action and, if I may be so bold as to suggest, because we have such low community standards of 'quality control' for the episodes that we realize. There are better ways of making episodes"* (Pearce, 2007b, p. 149). We need to mobilize all the practical wisdom and participatory knowledge that we have in order to act wisely in the particular situations of everyday life. Firstly, we can be careful in shaping our own contributions to speech acts. We can do this by offering utterances or actions that are easily arranged into constructive and respectful speech acts and by displaying social creativity to help recast events that seem to hold the potential of becoming offensive speech acts.

Secondly, we can pause and consider how our own punctuation of events is involved in shaping the moral force of common-sense logic that urges us to act in ways that might increase the risk of undesirable episodes. These considerations also involve challenging ourselves to imagine how different (mostly previous) punctuations might have helped create different and superior possibilities for action. And to completely abandon the blame game of common-sense logic which asks, "Who started it?" and "Who is to blame?" and instead seek to find a way to move forward together in a constructive manner.

Thirdly, we can pay more attention to how our own and others' utterances and speech acts contribute to shaping the plot in the stories that are told in organizations, including the way in which emplotment assigns roles to the individuals involved. Through this increased awareness we may be able to notice our own influence and choose to enable other emplotments and thus a better set of roles for ourselves and others.

Fourthly, we can enhance our sensitivity to the particularly crucial bifurcation points in the ongoing communication, where our choice of action has a significant impact on the subsequent course of events and our possibilities of constructing a better social world: *"Our social worlds are filled with conditions and patterns of interaction that no one would freely choose...This hypothesis implies that it doesn't help us to think of people who do bad things as bad people, or to attempt to correct intolerable conditions by removing the people responsible. A more effective way – if we can forgo our thirst to administer punishment – is to change the logical force that makes them think that they must do what they do. That is, if we think of people as players in various social games that make up our society, we would do better to change the games so that they have to play by different rules rather than convince them not to play or to play in such a way that they lose"* (Pearce, 2007b, p. 162). In other words: We are not simply at the mercy of other people. We can escape the moral force of common-sense logic by affecting the visible and less visible ground rules in our interactions.

Fifthly, we can do our best to create shared understandings of what is going on in the situations we enter into; i.e. a clear and common answer for everybody involved to the question, "What are we doing here and now?" As Peter Lang put it, *"When the context is unclear, you invite craziness into the room"* (personal conversation). Without a shared understanding of what it is we are doing, here and now, it is difficult and in some cases impossible to act in a meaningful way. Thus, social responsibility also involves enabling everybody involved to act as competent and morally responsible partici-pants.

In this chapter we have looked at linguistic philosophy and CMM theo-ry and introduced a number of key concepts and ideas with a view to illus-trating the complexity of the ongoing flow of events in organizations. It is one of the key points in the chapter that in order to understand interperson-al communication we do not need to *dive into* someone else's inner universe to achieve *deep* knowledge. Rather, we need to *dive into* the details of the micro-social processes of everyday patterns of communication in order to generate *useful* knowledge about the ongoing coordination of action and meaning. In the next chapter we examine the micro-social processes in the larger contexts of which they are part. Here, the movement is *outward* in order for us to grasp the big picture and examine how speech acts and episodes are also embedded in relationships, identity stories, the context of organizational culture, and the wider cultural context.

CHAPTER 4:

RELATIONSHIPS AND DIALOGIC OBLIGATIONS

In everyday language it is very common to talk about the "chemistry", the "climate", or the "atmosphere" in a team or an organization. We all know that this aspect must be in place for the sake of our well-being and our ability to cooperate with others. But what do these words refer to? One suggestion would be that we are trying to describe our relationships with others. As Kenneth J. Gergen emphasizes, we have a relatively limited vocabulary about our mutual relatedness, so we try to make sense by borrowing terms from the world of natural science (Gergen, 1994).

In this chapter, we want to focus on the connections between relational thinking and morality, based on inspiration from linguistic philosophy, moral philosophy, critical relational constructionism, narrative anthropological health care research, and the CMM theory.

One of the objectives of this chapter is to contribute to a richer language for relationships. We will be looking for useful terms that might heighten our awareness of our individual roles in co-creating relationships and enhance our social creativity. In everyday life in organizations, organizational members work together with many other people with whom they have a wide range of relationships. For the individual organizational member relationships may vary, for example with regard to how important, well defined, robust and harmonious they are. The complexity in organizations is associated with the myriad of relational patterns formed by the organizational members. Each manager, consultant and staff member is part of a unique relational pattern that is different from all the other organizational members' relational patterns and each member will have great difficulty grasping any other person's relational pattern.

As we briefly discussed in Chapter 2, it is a key feature of social constructionism to understand individuals in a relational perspective. That does not mean, however, that social constructionism is the only school of thought emphasizing relationships. Also, in realism, relationships are given an important role in human development and interpersonal communication. However, there are crucial differences between the two approaches. In realism, the individual comes before the relationship. In social constructionism, the relationship comes before the individual. We will elaborate on these differences later.

In this and the next chapter we will explore a social constructionist view of the individual. In this approach we are interested in exploring how a person's many selves are shaped, reshaped and vary with the many contexts and relationships in which the person is a part.

Some social constructionists want to avoid the term "self" altogether, as it invites a search for a person's stable and authentic "inner core". We opt for a plural form, saying that a person has many selves or identities that are displayed or performed depending on the context and relationship. In organizations there are many examples that a manager acts very competently in one department while failing completely at a later time in a different department. Or a staff member might produce stellar results in one project team but find no way to contribute in another team. Realism makes it difficult to offer a good explanation of these variations, since this epistemology views strong and weak points as stable properties in a person. That invites speculation that there is *something wrong* with the manager or the staff member. Maybe the person is sick? Under too much stress? Burned out? From a social constructionist perspective the changes give rise to a different set of questions – questions aimed at exploring contexts and relationships in the various situations.

In Chapter 3 we demonstrated how speech acts and episodes are shaped through everyday communicative micro-processes. Now, we will take a closer look at the subtle ways in which language acts to shape relationships.

THE RELATIONAL ROLE OF LANGUAGE

With regard to the role of language in relationships, social constructionism is again indebted to the linguistic philosopher John Austin, whose work we introduced in the previous chapter. In his book *How to Do Things with Words* Austin (1962) calls his theory a *theory of the language of actions*. In the same book Austin makes the interesting point that it is not enough to examine a speech act and its consequences. It is further necessary to insert a social "missing link" concerning the intention or obligation that the utterance expresses. Austin focuses on the social functions of speech acts. In addition to the words and their meaning, an utterance has a performative force (i.e. an utterance does something to relationships), especially as far as verbs are concerned.

Why is this interesting? If we take Austin's idea a few steps further it becomes clear that the choice of verbs has considerable impact on what happens between people. Verbs help define the parties' moral obligations and entitlements and implicitly shape mutual expectations. Certain verbs are likely to generate unequal relationships where one party is one up. Examples are the verbs "diagnose", "characterize" and "warn". Other verbs serve the social function of strengthening the mutual relatedness between people (e.g. the verbs "promise", "approve" and "apologize"). A third category of verbs can be viewed as instruments of meta-communication, that is, a means of clarifying what sort of communication in which the parties are engaged, such as "inform", "describe" and "tell". Thus, as we speak we are constantly shaping our relationships with others through subtle details in the language we use. As we also pointed out in the previous chapter, all organizational members thus have a shared responsibility for the resulting events.

Austin's work also illustrates how power and morality are embedded in language. However, Austin's linguistic philosophy was developed in the context of the English language. He was a philosopher – not an anthropologist or social psychologist. Therefore, he did not address whether the English verbs would have the same social meaning in other cultures, or how they might vary depending on the context within the same culture. That was not what he set out to do. However, it is part of our purpose, so let us now turn to these questions.

CULTURE AND ETHICS

Throughout the 1900s, research findings from anthropological and ethnographic studies have served as an important source of inspiration for the development of social constructionism and communication theory. Cross-cultural comparisons have proved a fruitful way of taking a fresh look at one's own culture. Thus, we will now venture on a longer detour through

some researchers' considerations about how to make sure it is ethically justifiable to carry out health care research projects in foreign cultures. The
researchers are Americans who have been in charge of research projects in
the East, in Eastern Europe and in black subcultures in the United States
over the years. The researchers' own moral dilemmas have made a great
impression on us, and we hope that this detour will help clarify some key
points about how culture acts as an often invisible backdrop for "obvious
truths" about ethics and morality.

In 2005, the journal: Health: *The Interdisciplinary Journal of the Social Study
of Health, Illness and Medicine* published a special issue on *Ethics, Informed
Consent and Narrative*. The idea had arisen after a conference in 2001 when
some of the speakers met at a Greek restaurant in Cambridge. In the introduction to the special issue, the two editors, Catherine Kohler Riessman and
Cheryl Mattingly, describe the restaurant visit, and the reader senses that the
mood was not high, but highly pensive. After the lectures there had been
persistent questions about whether the ethical guidelines of the institutional review board had been adhered to. Had the respondents in fact offered
their informed consent? Had confidentiality actually been preserved? Had
the researchers displayed respect for the respondents' privacy? Etc. Before
the dinner was over, the small group had reached the conclusion that
although these questions were extremely relevant, they were posed within a
narrow framework where the respondents' individual rights were the pre-
dominant focus and without any awareness of the cultural context that the
respondents were part of. The line of thinking that the questions reflected
was characterized by the medical/scientific approach, but was that really relevant for ethnographic and narrative approaches to health care research?

They decided the answer was no and set out to study the complex connections between the ethical domain of informed consent and narrative approaches to research.

The project turned out to take four years. But the result was excellent. As an example we will first look at an article written by Catherine Kohler Riessman (2005), who is a research professor in the Department of Sociology at Boston University. One of the persistent themes in her research is narrative descriptions of "biographical disruption", that is, life stories involving events that have disrupted and radically altered the narrators' expectations of continuity in their lives. These disruptions and changes in course might involve divorce, chronic illness or childlessness. In her article in Health she writes about a research project in a medical clinic that offers treatment to young couples who cannot have children. The clinic is in Kerala in southern India. The research project was carried out in 1993-1994 and was subject to the institutional review board's usual ethical guidelines about informed consent, respect for the respondents' privacy, research neutrality, etc. Below, we include a paraphrased excerpt of Riessman's account of some of the ethical considerations emerging in this research project.

STORY 3: THE RESEARCHER'S MORAL DILEMMAS IN AN UNFAMILIAR CULTURE

My research project was about the meaning and handling of childlessness – an invisible problem in India, where the government has a population policy that aimed to keep birth rates down. My research application was kept in a detached language intended for the evaluators on the institutional review board in the United States. The application also included a consent form to be filled out and signed by the prospective respondents in accordance with common procedures for sociological research. At the time I did not question these procedures.

It was not long after my arrival in Kerala before the first hint of trouble appeared. My local research assistant expressed very polite reservations about the informed consent form and told me that "we don't do that here." I interviewed childless women in cities, villages and in the fertility clinic, where they came in as patients. Many signed the informed consent form, but a significant number of women were reluctant to sign their names. It turned out that they associated official documents with government authorities. Signing documents in an Indian context carried with it a history of central power and its intrusion into local life, and thus it took on a meaning that was completely different from the intention of protecting respondents, that was embedded in the Western culture and its discourse on research ethics. The power aspect became clearer to me: Consent forms serve to protect the university and the research sponsors from liability and to transfer the ownership of information from participant to researcher.

Another moral problem had to do with confidentiality. In Western research it is essential that the respondent provide information in a space of confidentiality. That is only possible if a situation is established where the researcher can interview the participants one on one. Let me use the interview with Celine as an example. Celine was a 26-year-old woman who suffered greatly because she did not have a child. She and her husband lived in a village together with her family – parents and sisters. It proved very difficult to speak with Celine one on one, since both family members and neighbors clustered about us, and family members would expand on Celine's answers. Confidentiality does not make any sense in a public space, so how could I live up to this requirement?

Our conversations soon became saturated with conflicting expectations and assumptions. Celine and her family took part in the project in the expectation of receiving something in return that might fix her problem of childlessness. I discovered that they viewed me as a gynecologist, even though I had introduced myself as a sociologist, and after a while they asked whether I had reached a diagnosis, and whether I would be taking the information to the hospital. It took me a long time to understand that assurances of confidentiality were irrelevant to them – or maybe even a disappointment. From my point of view I entered into a relationship with them based on a desire to generate new knowledge about childlessness as a social problem – not as a medical problem. My purpose was to contribute to a social critique. The woman and her family wanted help with a problem that they viewed as medical– a fault in her body – and they expected that I would be able to act to fix this fault.

This revealed another cultural difference. Informed consent, confidentiality and respect for privacy as ethical ground rules for a relationship that aims to generate new knowledge require that the respondent and the researcher have a shared concept of "research". I do not think that my informants did. They must have been very confused as to what it was all about.

Looking back now, I am troubled by our failures of communication. The experience gave rise to unsettling emotions that have since urged me to ponder the moral issues of power and unclear contexts and relationships associated with research. That raises the fundamental question of whether the potential benefit of a research project can possibly compensate for the inequality and the uncertainty as to morality and ethics.

In the closing section of her article, Riessman writes that she finds it important for researchers to contribute with their personal stories about their experiences, ethical reflections and moral decisions in real-life situations: *"Linking experience and reflection, I begin to question taken-for-granted, socially constructed categories – informed consent, patient autonomy and respect, privacy and confidentiality – the techno-speak of institutional review boards. Rather than writing in the propositional voice of mainstream scholarship, I chose narrative – another way of knowing"* (Riessman, 2005, p.486).

The moral dilemmas are particularly striking when research is done with a narrative approach, where informants contribute with their life stories, which through the researcher's questions come to contain a wealth of concrete information about individuals, places, times, etc. How is it possible to draw a line around privacy when the object of study is a life story? The telling of a life story requires a special relationship between researcher and respondent. This relationship must be characterized by trust, respect and equality. If that is the case, Riessman underlines, it is difficult for the researcher to take his or her own presence out of the equation, as required in traditional scientific research with the purpose of ensuring objectivity. Instead, the researcher should give up his or her position as a detached, separate and objective observer and allow his or her emotions to serve as a guide: *"Emotions served as warnings, red flags about what deeply mattered"* and later, *"Abstract rules did not help me, when I was in ethical trouble"* (Riessman, 2005, p. 486). The ethical guidelines of the institutional review board were no help when her emotions indicated that the relationships were troubled. Riessman concludes that it is profoundly problematic to transfer ethical principles unmodified from one culture to another. What is required is *"an ethics-in-context grounded in the exigencies of specific settings."*

The entire special issue of the journal directs severe criticism at both the practice and the thinking associated with the way institutional review boards define ethical guidelines. In the article *"Toward a vulnerable ethics of research practice"* another contributor to the special issue, Cheryl Mattingly (2005), a professor of anthropology at the University of Southern California, discusses the implicit assumptions on which the review boards base their thinking. Briefly put, these assumptions are:

1. It is possible to articulate universal ethical principles or guidelines that are useful in every situation. Ethical rules are context-free.
2. There is always an ethical "right answer".
3. There is an objective position from which to judge what one ought to do. This position is characterized by an emotional detachment from the situation.
4. This objectively defined position, without any emotional involvement, enables the articulation of unambiguous ethical guidelines.

With examples from her own research, Mattingly illustrates in a highly thought-provoking way the shortcomings of these assumptions. Insightful descriptions from a variety of cultural contexts demonstrate that it is extremely problematic to imagine that complex moral dilemmas can be resolved within the framework of a single set of standards. A signature on a consent form is considered an agreement between researcher and respondent ensuring that the researcher acts in an ethically justifiable way. But a relationship cannot be defined once and for all on the basis of a formal document. As a life story unfolds the relationship changes, and new expectations arise for the respondent – expectations that are often incompatible with the researcher's role as a neutral and detached observer. The previously mentioned study on childlessness in Kerala, India serves as a good illustration of this phenomenon.

In some cases the principle of privacy can become a lack of respect for the respondent. Mattingly's research dealt with terminally ill patients' and their encounter with the hospital system. She emphasizes that marginalized persons can have a great desire for others to learn from their profoundly traumatic experiences in their encounters with treatment professionals. They do not want confidentiality; on the contrary, they want their stories to be made public – with inclusion of their names, if possible – to make their voices heard in society. Sticking to the requirement for confidentiality robs them of a voice and fails to acknowledge the value of their life experience.

Therefore, Mattingly concludes that it is crucial to find new ways for the researcher's ethical considerations – ways that lead away from the universal principles and guidelines and toward the articulation of narrative ethics. The key objective must be to discover what constitutes "the good" in a unique and specific situation. The only way for us to answer this question is to explore what stories the individuals see themselves as being part of, which relationships they are part of, and what future they are trying to build.

In recent decades there has been growing interest within some professional communities (social workers, nurses, psychologists, etc.) and associations to articulate ethical guidelines. Using such a set of ethical principles or guidelines in a practical organizational context comes with considerable challenges. Here we share the above mentioned researchers' concerns for the impact that such guidelines might have on the shaping of contexts and relationships. We will now continue to explore how relationships and identity stories are co-created. And we will return to the organizational setting.

SHIFTING LEVELS OF CONTEXT

Culture casts a certain light on the possible meanings of the relationship between researcher and respondent and the situations that unfold in a cross-cultural research practice. The contextual force from the two different cultures, that researcher and respondent belong to, generates conflicting views of the relationship and of the many small actions that are involved in Western research practices (reading the consent form, explaining the respondent's rights, signing, choosing a private space for the interview, etc.). Using Austin's terminology, we can say that in this setting with a clash between divergent cultural norms it was not possible to create successful speech acts and mutually compatible stories about episodes.

We will now return to the CMM theory and to how the continuous flow of myriad tiny utterances and actions in everyday life is arranged into speech acts, and how speech acts are arranged into stories about episodes. An important point is the reciprocal influence between different *levels of context*: Speech act, episode, identity, relationship(s), organizational culture, and culture. The contextual force from a higher level of context, such as organizational culture, to a lower level, such as an episode, generates certain possibilities for the construction of meaning and rules out others. Western culture contains certain dominant stories about the relationship between manager and employee that frame the interaction, but within this framework there is room for many variations. We shall return to this variation in the chapter 5.

Meanwhile, a lower level of context has an upward force on a higher level, for instance when an episode transforms a relationship in a particular way: Recurring episodes where a manager criticizes a staff member will affect the relationship between manager and employee.

We will now bring these ideas into play in our next story. The situation is an evaluation meeting, which is specified in the narrator's contract to take place after a three-month trial period. The outcome of the evaluation meeting will determine whether the narrator is offered a permanent position. The narrator is a young psychologist, Marianne. This was her second position after graduation. Her first job was a six-month temporary position in an HR-function.

STORY 4: TRIAL PERIOD EVALUATION TURNED THERAPY

I was so excited when I managed to find a new job just one month after my first temp position ended. It was a consultancy job in a private company – my dream job with interesting assignments and a professional environment that included several other psychologists – among them, my boss. And it was a permanent position!

On one of the first days of my new job I was told that the arrangement called for a three-month trial period. The date of the trial period evaluation had already been written into my calendar.

When the day arrived I was told five minutes before the meeting that three of my coworkers would take part in the meeting. That was a bit of a surprise to me. I thought that a trial period evaluation would be a conversation between a manager and an employee, but that was not the way they did it here. The conversation took place in a meeting room, and when I came in my boss was seated at the end of the meeting table and the three coworkers along one side. I was seated on the other side and said, "Wow, this looks like an examination!" No reply. The first thing that happened was that my boss asked me if I would like to speak first. I was a bit unclear as to how I was supposed to proceed, so I spoke loosely about my work tasks and my relations with my coworkers; in both of these areas I thought that things were going really well.

At this point my boss interrupted and said that she would like to explain why she had hired me. Now followed a long list of plus-words: dynamic, theoretically well founded, competent, etc. I was just waiting for the "but". And there it was: "But you are showing a great deal of personal confidence!" said the boss. One of my coworkers added her bit: "Yes, we've talked about that too; for example you don't seem the slightest bit nervous when you have to present something to a large audience". I agreed that I was in fact not nervous in these situations, in part because in my previous job I had done a number of consultancy tasks, so I was quite experienced with speaking to groups. "But you must be slightly nervous, and if you're not it must be because you are not in touch with your emotions," my boss said. My other coworkers also provided examples of my excessive personal confidence, and I could tell that this was something they had discussed in advance. I was shocked and said that I was listening but did not wish to respond because I found the topic far too private.

My boss then said that she was convinced that this was an important area of development for me – an area that probably reflected a troubling personal history. She emphasized the importance that I address my lack of nervousness – for my own sake as well as others', as my confidence might scare others off. My boss assured me that she was prepared to assist in my personal development.

The whole thing was intensely unpleasant for me. I felt humiliated and violated. I could not believe that a conversation about work-related topics had suddenly turned into questions about my private feelings and life story.

I tried to end the conversation by saying that I felt that they were locking me into a place where I did not wish to be.

My boss again emphasized how important it was for me to work on my personal development and to get more in touch with my emotions. It takes a lot to shock me, but this conversation shocked me. It seemed I had to be a completely different person. At this point the meeting had lasted about an hour and a half, and no one had brought up anything relating to how I was handling my work assignments. That was actually what I thought the meeting was going to focus on.

My boss then said that it was time to end the meeting. I managed to say that I had been paying attention to what they were saying, but that I wanted to be who I was.

What is going on here? We do not know how the manager experienced the situation, since we only know the story from Marianne's point of view. However, we will venture a few hypotheses about the possible assumptions that might make her actions meaningful. It is clear from the story that the manager is a psychologist. If she is inspired by traditional psychology with a focus on the individual's inner life, she may have concluded that Marianne's confident appearance is only a front, beneath which lies far greater insecurity than Marianne is prepared to acknowledge. Perhaps the manager thinks that she would like to help Marianne realize the truth about herself and address this important area of development that Marianne seems to be unaware of. As a psychologist the manager probably also feels that she is on safe ground professionally, and she may feel convinced that she is not only entitled, but indeed *obligated* to share her interpretations with Marianne.

From Marianne's point of view the conversation starts out as an evaluation of her work performance, where the episode is the overall context, and the relationship between manager and employee is secondary. The episode of a work-related context matches the definition of the relationship as that of manager and employee. However, the manager's statements about the employee's need for personal development and her offer of assistance with this endeavor lead to a shift of context for the employee: that is, her self-conception becomes the highest context. At the same time, it becomes unclear what sort of relationship is being shaped, and what sort of episode is unfolding. When the context of both relationship and episode becomes unclear, communication is severely hampered. As we saw, the employee chose to declare that she did not want to contribute.

We may guess that this trial period evaluation left the employee very uncertain as to how she should label her relationship with her manager, and how she was supposed to behave within this relationship. Was the manager acting as a therapist? A superior? A friend? A relationship between a therapist and a client is subject to very different ethical ground rules than that between a manager and an employee. An unclear context makes it difficult for the two parties to coordinate their actions. It is part of the story that Marianne subsequently made a deliberate effort to talk to her boss as a manager rather than a psychologist or a therapist in order to reestablish a manager-employee relationship. This effort was sufficiently successful for Marianne to decide to stay in the job.

What we say in a given situation has a creative power in terms of shaping episodes and relationships. As we saw in the beginning of this chapter, one little verb has the power to shape a relationship between people. So do other categories of words. In the public debate about integration policies in Denmark, one of the debaters recently pointed to an interesting example of the power of language to shape relationships. In the United States children and young people who are born in the United States by immigrant parents are typically referred to as *first-generation Americans*. In Denmark, we speak of *first-*, *second-* and *third-generation immigrants*. These Danish expressions, which are very common, have a significant impact on the way in which we cast the relationship between *third-generation immigrants* and *Danes* as a relationship between *the foreigners* and *us* or between *them* and *us*. The terms create a gap and unequal opportunities of being part of society. It is highly likely that this definition of a relationship also helps create stories of identity that cast new citizens as *deviant* and ethnic Danes as *normal*. This is an example of the social constructionist point about the close link between relationship and identity.

Recently, a more respectful expression has begun to gain ground in Denmark: *New Danes*. Hopefully, the relationship between 'Danes' and 'New Danes' can be more mutually respectful than that between 'Danes' and 'second- or third-generation immigrants'.

As a member of an organization one is at any given moment part of a complex relational pattern that is difficult to grasp. Our relationships with others in organizations are created, recreated and reshaped in an ongoing flow of events affected by the micro-processes of communication. The next chapter examines *how* discourses and narratives create relationships. But first, we will look at two different approaches to relationships. As we mentioned in the beginning of this chapter the term *relationship* is applied differently depending on the theory and epistemology at play.

TWO APPROACHES TO RELATIONAL THINKING

In Chapter 2 we offered an initial introduction to some of the most important differences between key concepts in realism and social constructionism. Here, we take a closer look at some points of view that are particularly relevant for relational thinking.

How can we conceptualize different types of relationships in organizations or different ways of shaping relationships? These two versions of what is almost the same question illustrate two different approaches to understanding relationships. How organizational members understand the concept of relationships plays an important role in their decisions and actions; both in everyday communication and in HR and management practices. The following discussion is based on an important book: *The Social Construction of Organizations*, which is the result of collaboration between Dian Marie Hosking, a professor of relational processes at Utrecht University School of Governance in the Netherlands, and Sheila McNamee, a professor of communication at New Hampshire University in the United States (Hosking & McNamee, 2006).

Hosking describes how she - at the beginning of her career of teaching organizational theory - soon discovered that most of the literature treats individuals and organizations as if they were separate and well-defined entities that can be described in themselves, independent of one another. Viewing people as autonomous individuals affects our understanding of relationships. The ground is ripe for a view of subject-object relationships where an individual is defined as the subject, while other individuals are defined as objects. An example of a subject-object relationship is that between an agent of change (the subject = the agent) and an affected party (the object). This example and others will be discussed in the next chapter.

With inspiration from both the CMM theory and Hosking's critical relational constructionism the figure below illustrates the two approaches to relational thinking.

Figure 2: Two Approaches to Relational Thinking

	REALISM	SOCIAL CONSTRUCTIONISM
FOCUS ON	The individual as an entity	The relationship between ourselves and others as the entity
EVENTS ARE THE RESULT OF	Individual actions	Patterns of coordination
RELATIONSHIPS ARE VIEWED AS	Objects that can be described	Processes that create people and realities
RELATIONSHIPS ARE	External and instrumental	Embedded in narratives
UNDERSTANDING RELATIONSHIPS IS A MATTER OF	Uncovering and describing pre-existing relationships	Exploring the processes of co-creation in which relationships are created and changed on an ongoing basis
CHARACTERISTICS OF THE RELATIONSHIP	Subject-object Hierarchical/ vertical	Subject-subject Horizontal
POWER	Power over others	Influence on defining "reality"
PRODUCTION OF KNOWLEDGE	Spectator knowledge Expert knowledge	Participatory knowledge Relational insight

Most comparisons in the table sum up previous sections. A couple of the points, however, deserve to be unfolded.

One of Hosking's interesting points addresses how the understanding of relationships differs between realism and social constructionism. The former suggests that the relationship is shaped as a subject-object relationship where the subject is "one up" in relation to the object, while the latter suggests that the relationship is shaped as a subject-subject relationship, where the parties are on the same level.

Hosking suggests how power is constructed in the two lines of thinking. In the subject-object relationship the subject aims to gain power over the object, while power in a subject-subject relationship is about how the ongoing communication leads to knowledge being credited or discredited, demands for identity being seen as more or less legitimate, possibilities opening up or shutting down, and the participants being assigned or barred from certain positions. Thus, in this line of thinking, power is understood as influence on how "reality" is defined (Hosking, 2006). The author's ideas on this topic are an extension of Pearce's ideas about the construction of meaning as the result of the coordination of many actors' actions. Definitions of what constitutes "reality" are the result of co-creation.

Both types of relationships produce knowledge. In the subject-object relationship the subject learns about the object; in the subject-subject relationship both (all) parties may gain greater insight. Pearce's concepts of spectator knowledge and participatory knowledge, which we discussed in Chapter 3, are also useful here. In the subject-object relationship the subject may be, for example, an expert advisor who uses linear methods to increase his or her expert knowledge about another human being as an object. These methods will be characterized by one-way communication and organized in stages: first information gathering, then processing, and finally the presentation of findings (Haslebo & Nielsen, 2000). The expert advisor thus gathers information about the object (spectator knowledge). This creates a vertical and alienating relationship.

In subject-subject relationships there is a growth in relational insight, that is, insight into how the actors co-create each other and each other's conditions for success. The actors co-create participatory knowledge that can be meaningful and useful for both.

Figure 2 summarizing the two approaches to relational thinking illustrates an inspirational point: Our basic assumptions about the individual, the construction of events, and the production of knowledge affect the relationships we build with others: There is a close link between concepts of relationship and everyday practices. Let us therefore take a closer look at how both subject-object and subject-subject relationships are shaped in the micro-processes of communication.

CHARACTERISTICS OF SUBJECT-OBJECT RELATIONSHIPS IN ORGANIZATIONS

Hosking describes four characteristics of a subject-object relationship.

Firstly, the *subject is positioned as active and the object as passive*. The subject is seen as the person who actively generates knowledge about the object; the object is viewed as an entity about which it is possible to know more. The praxis in which the parties are engaged is about uncovering, examining and describing characteristics of the object. The subject is viewed as the knowing party and the object as the entity that it is important to gather knowledge about. This may apply to the relationship between a researcher and a respondent or between a manager and a job applicant. The subject may also be active in the sense that he or she is responsible for correctly diagnosing the object based on his or her knowledge of methods that are considered appropriate for producing objective knowledge within the given field of knowledge.

Secondly, a subject-object relationship aims to *explain the relationship based on personal characteristics of the subject and the object*. These characteristics are attributed a causal role. A hostile relationship, for example, can be explained by assumptions of aggressive motives or malevolent intentions. A manager's success in generating team spirit can be explained, for example, with reference to his or her personal charisma.

Thirdly, the *subject is positioned as affecting, and the object as affected*. The subject exercises this influence based on his or her knowledge. To a manager, therefore, the key is to constantly gain more knowledge about the individual employees and to make sure that this knowledge is correct and adequate. It is assumed that thorough knowledge about the employees is an important condition for the manager to act rationally and affect the employees efficiently. In a subject-object relationship the subject aims to gain power over the object.

Fourthly, subject-object thinking leads the subject to *consider the relationship as instrumental*. A good relationship becomes a tool that the subject can use to reach his or her goals. Sales and marketing often involve organizational practices based on a subject-object perception. A statement such as, *"A good relationship with the customer enables added sales,"* stems from a view of the customer as an object and the relationship as instrumental. Many of the concepts and activities initiated by HR departments position managers and employees as objects that are targeted by the HR consultants' development efforts. This is a point that we will explore in more depth in the following chapters.

DIALOGIC OBLIGATIONS

Shaping relationships between organizational members as subject-object relationships reduces the likelihood of mutually respectful communication. Thus, subject-subject relationships can be considered mutually respectful relationships, while subject-object relationships cannot.

Now, we can view the moral dilemmas facing researchers and managers in this light. The researchers in Story 3 (page 106) became increasingly aware that narrative approaches to research were incompatible with a subject-object relationship between a researcher and a respondent. They saw how the ethical guidelines that are common in the research world promoted the formation of a subject-object relationship. A signature on a consent form did not safeguard the moral treatment of respondents; that would require an ongoing dialogue where the researchers took an interest in the respondents' cultural background. The researchers also suggested that an ongoing dialogue would be able to reshape a subject-object relationship into a more mutually respectful relationship. However, that would require them to suspend the general ethical guidelines of the review boards and instead turn their attention not only to the cultural background but also to the specific context of the conversation and the particular ethical considerations to which it gives rise.

In the first review of Story 2: *Friendly Concern or Sexual Harassment?* in Chapter 3 we saw how one e-mail: "I saw you in the lunch room. You looked so sad. Is there anything I can do for you?" was arranged into a speech act that was labeled an *improper advance*. We also toyed with the idea of Diane contacting Hank directly and the resulting opportunity for them to arrange the e-mail into different speech acts. The story of sexual harassment, however, relieved Diane of the moral obligation to engage in dialogue, which her manager confirmed by not arranging a meeting with Hank and his manager.

The social constructionist perspective of the concept of relationships, however, necessitates the moral obligation to engage in dialogue. It is not enough to be convinced that one has worked everything out – in one's own mind. We have to engage in dialogue. Dialogue is not just a conversation; it is a conversation with a particular quality. The word *dialog* comes from the Greek *dia*, which means between or through, and *logos*, which means word or knowledge. The original meaning of the word is a process that generates knowledge. There is more to the word dialogue than simply *two-way communication* (which Pearce's quote below elaborates on). What, then, do dialogic obligations imply? Here, we will highlight three important aspects:

Firstly, it implies a moral obligation to engage in *direct contact* with the involved individuals, that is, to talk *with* others rather than *about* them. That takes personal courage and social imagination. In organizations, members spend a great deal of time talking *about* others. This occurs in management teams, for example, where managers exchange stories about what their staff members "are like". It also happens in informal situations when organizational members meet to vent. Venting is a form of communication that is known and practiced in most organizations. In many cases, organization members are convinced that venting is a necessary outlet for their many grievances. Seen in a social constructionist light, venting probably serves to perpetuate these grievances: We strengthen the aspects and features that we pay attention to (see Chapter 6). However, venting also has implications for the relationships in the organization. Venting often involves discussing someone, for example, managers, who are not present. That defines the relationships between the "venters" and the person(s) in question as subject-object relationships, which will hamper the establishment of future respectful communication and make it harder to resolve the problems that the "venters" are experiencing.

Secondly, dialogic obligations involve *paying attention to the mutual relatedness* and to the mutual character of the meaning-constructing processes in organizations. Individual acts or utterances do not have meaning in themselves. This point implies a moral challenge to avoid stigmatizing others, to avoid moral judgment and quick retaliation and instead find the time and the opportunity to consider one's own role in shaping contexts and relationships.

Thirdly, dialogic obligations require the individual organizational member to *put an effort into the way they communicate*. In his 2007 book, Pearce uses the following definition of dialogue: *"I'm using a technical sense of 'dialogue' here. I do not mean just talk. Rather, I'm referring to a particular quality of communication in which a relationship is formed in which each participant remains in the tension between standing your ground and being profoundly open to the others. ... In dialogic communication, it makes sense to say 'We disagree? Wonderful! How did you come to hold your position?' Dialogic conversations enlarge perspectives rather than constrict them; enable us to discover more about our own positions than we had originally known; permit us to address the 'gray areas' as well as the things about which we are certain; and paradoxically, in the absence of the attempt to persuade, we often come to agree with each other"* (Pearce, 2007b, p. 215).

Stewart and Zediker (2002) define dialogue as a particularly tensional moral practice. They prefer to reserve the term *dialogue* for the moments when the parties succeed in remaining in a tensional conversation where they simultaneously articulate their own moral points of view and expose themselves to others' points of views. Dialogue with this quality contains a transformative power that is capable of changing both the parties' understanding and their mutual relationship.

Dialogue requires that the participants assume an orientation that is characterized by openness, curiosity and willingness to explore their own as well as the other person's points of view. Openness, curiosity and the manner of inquiry, however, also vary with one's conception of relationship. With inspiration from Winslade and Monk's (2001) work on mediation we have set up the comparison illustrated in Figure 3 between two very different approaches.

Figure 3: Two Approaches to Inquiry

REALISM	SOCIAL CONSTRUCTIONISM
Asking questions to confirm or dismiss one's own hypotheses	Asking questions from a position of not-knowing
Inviting the other person into a position of an object that one wants to know something about	Inviting the other person into a position as a knowing subject
Asking questions to collect pieces of information	Asking questions to shed light on potential connections
Appreciating precise definitions	Appreciating ambiguity and wonder
Interpreting the other person's answers in the light of general knowledge	Exploring the other person's version of reality
Asking questions to identify key causal factors	Asking questions to expand the scope of possibility
Asking questions about the ordinary aspects of everyday events	Asking questions about the extraordinary aspects of everyday events
Asking questions in order to arrive at a diagnosis	Asking questions to help create a new understanding of how to move forward

In the framework of realism, questions are phrased around pre-determined hypotheses with a view to enabling the questioner to do an analysis and reach a conclusion. The person who has to answer the questions often experiences the situation as an investigation or an interrogation. The field of conversation is restricted. Cooperrider (2001) characterizes this line of questioning as *the paralysis of analysis*. Within the framework of social constructionism the goal is to engage in an explorative dialogue. This topic will be unfolded in Chapter 6, which deals with appreciation and inquiry of value to the work community. Here the key point is that we shape relationships through the way in which we communicate. Of course, communication consists of much more than questions. Here, however, we illustrate the point through the two very different approaches to asking questions. The epistemology of realism makes it natural to ask linear questions with the characteristics outlined in Figure 3. Linear questions tend to shape the relationship between the questioner and the other person as a subject-object relationship, while the formation of a subject-subject relationship requires that both parties master the art of dialogue and take turns asking questions and offering preliminary answers based on a shared awareness that creating a better social world is a shared responsibility.

REFLECTIONS

In this chapter we have discussed some complex connections between language, cultural context, relationships and forms of communication. The idea that language is involved in shaping the relationships we are part of was illustrated with Austin's detailed efforts to analyze the power of verbs to shape relationships.

Next, we went on to demonstrate how words also take their meaning from the cultural context. With examples from anthropological research inspired by narrative approaches we concluded that general ethical guidelines are not enough to safeguard the moral treatment of the respondents who take part in a research project. In fact, such guidelines may even contribute to shaping subject-object relationships between researchers and respondents, where the respondent is denied a voice and the opportunity to share the value of his or her own life experiences. The cultural context and the micro-processes of the conversational context are crucial for the parties' ability to co-create a communication that respects relational ethics.

The concept of relationships is understood in many different ways within various theoretical frameworks. The choice of either realism or social constructionism as one's conceptual basis has a profound impact on our understanding of relationships. The main differences were summarized in Figure 2. Realism shapes relationships as subject-object relationships. Many of the HR activities and practices in use in organizations lead to the formation of subject-object relationships. This applies, for example, to management development methods such as the 360-degree appraisal, which we will discuss in Chapter 7. In the next chapter we demonstrate how effective some of the culturally dominant discourses are in placing organizational members in particular positions and creating subject-object relationships.

Dialogic obligations, which are crucial for promoting subject-subject relationships, imply a moral obligation to talk *with the persons involved* and to avoid talking *about* them in situations where they are not present. It also requires an awareness of the mutual relatedness in organizations as well as considerable skill and care in the way we communicate. Effective dialogue is a challenging skill that *requires appreciation of the other*. The concept of appreciation will be explored more in depth in Chapter 6. Dialogue and appreciation go hand in hand and pave the way for mutually respectful relationships. As a preliminary, however, we need to establish the concepts of positioning and discourse, which will be the topic of the next chapter.

CHAPTER 5

DISCOURSE AND THE SHARED RESPONSIBILITY FOR POSITIONING

What we take for granted in our culture often finds its way into our organizations and affects the construction and the quality of our organizational relationships. In this chapter we take a closer look at positioning theory and examine how historically and culturally shaped discourses provide material for narratives and thus contribute to placing organizational members in positions that shape relationships, often in unnoticeable ways.

We will also offer our view of the link between positioning theory and CMM theory. In chapter 3 we illustrated how speech acts, episodes and narrative plots affect each other. In the present chapter we take a closer look at positioning by narrative plots, and how conversations between organizational members position managers and employees in certain ways – and not always attractive ways. In the words of narrative-inspired writers and practitioners John Winslade and Gerald Monk: "*In each utterance we make in a conversation, we offer others positions from which they may relate to us. We issue them position calls. ... We can think of these positions as participants' physical orientations to each other that express relational influence; that authorize the other to speak or not to speak, or to speak only in certain terms; that allow what we say to count or not count; or that limit or widen our possibilities for acting in our own worlds. This is the sense in which language, as Bronwyn Davies suggests, speaks us into existence and constitutes our personhood, as we use it to communicate with others"* (Winslade & Monk, 2001, p. 121). This quote illustrates an important point in a view of relationships that is inspired by social constructionism: In conversations we not only speak based on "who we are"; we speak from the position we are temporarily invited into and occupying. It is in this sense that the relationship comes before the individual, as we mentioned in the previous chapter.

For the present chapter we have selected a couple of culturally generated discourses that greatly affect how managers, consultants and employees can create meaning and coordinate their actions with each other. Our reason for focusing on these particular discourses is that they are both widespread and very powerful – a power that promotes positioning that locks the parties into non-respectful relationships and restricts their scope of possible actions. The way in which we issue positioning invitations in everyday conversations is not just a technical communication issue but also a highly moral issue. Thus, we will first explore the connection between positioning and ethics.

POSITIONING AND ETHICS

Positioning theory is a seminal theory with new concepts that can help us understand one of the key but abstract ideas in social constructionism, which is that the individual's identity, self-conception or selves are shaped in the relationships in which he or she participates.

Positioning is about the linguistic processes in ongoing communication that help place the persons in certain positions rather than others.

Positioning takes place in discourses. A *discourse* is a rather difficult concept that is best understood as culturally familiar narratives that define certain positions and relationships as obvious or natural at the exclusion of others (Burr, 1999). In Western culture, for example, a discourse on the treatment of disease will place the parties in the positions of doctor, patient, researcher or layperson. An annual appraisal review can be seen as a socially and organizationally defined discourse that offers the positions of manager or employee.

The dominant discourse on the necessity of personal development defines the actors as therapist and client. The manager in Story 4: *Trial Period Evaluation turned Therapy*, may have found inspiration for her positioning in the conversation from this discourse (see Chapter 4). The position that we are each assigned or which we assign to ourselves or "negotiate" in the discourse shapes our self-conception. In the story mentioned above, the "negotiation" about positions failed at first, as the employee did not wish to accept the client position.

Burr (1999) explains this important point about the connection between positioning, relationship and identity as follows: *"Positions in discourse are also seen as providing us with the content of our subjectivity. Once we take up a position within a discourse (and some of these positions entail a long-term occupation by the person, like gender or fatherhood), we then inevitably come to experience the world and ourselves from the vantage point of that perspective. Once we take up a subject position in discourse, we have available to us a particular, limited set of concepts, images, metaphors, ways of speaking, self-narratives and so on that we take on as our own"* (Burr, 1995, p. 145).

How does this happen? We will take a closer look at that question by considering the following story.

STORY 5: THE COURSE PARTICIPANT WHO WAS INVITED TO SHARE PRIVATE INFORMATION

A group of colleagues were gathered one day to discuss their future cooperation. About half the group worked together on a daily basis, while the others worked in different locations around the country. Some had travelled far to arrive that same morning. Therefore the consultant who was hired to facilitate the process opened with a check-in, that is, a method to help the participants "arrive" in the room. The consultant asked the participants to stand in a circle. Then he placed a tennis ball on the floor in the middle of the circle and said, "Now, someone please pick up the ball and say a few words about where you're at right now. Then throw the ball to someone else, who will say a few words about where they're at right now. Only the person who has the ball is allowed to speak." There were a few questions to clarify what he meant by "where you're at right now", and the consultant explained that the term should not be taken literally but was more about what was on one's mind, how one felt, etc. After some hesitation the exercise slowly got started. One participant said that he felt a bit rushed and had almost missed his very early morning train. Someone else said that she had really been looking forward to this day and meeting her new colleagues, while a third person said that her muscles were quite sore because she and her boyfriend were fixing up their new house.

Then the ball was thrown to a fourth colleague, Bob, who said that he was preoccupied with the fact that his daughter had been hospitalized the day before because she was pregnant and had pelvic pains. "And it's her first child, well, and my first grandchild and it was difficult for them to conceive, so ... so that's weighing heavily on my mind, and during the breaks I'll probably be making phone calls. So if you see me looking a bit absent-minded today, it's probably because I'm thinking about that ..." As he was telling this, there were sounds of support and compassion from the others.

The consultant thanked him for sharing and otherwise let the process continue with ball-throwing and monologues. One of the next colleagues said that she really appreciated hearing what Bob had said, since now she knew how he felt, and what was going on if he seemed a little pre-occupied at times. Then she expressed her compassion with the difficult situation he was in.

When everybody had spoken, it was time for a break. Bob immediately went to see the consultant and said that he felt it was a very unpleasant activity, and that he had felt coaxed into sharing something that was far too private, and which he now regretted saying. It had bothered him a great deal to suddenly be the object of his coworkers' pity. The comment that now they knew how he felt had bothered him in particular. He was also angry that he had not been given a proper chance to make a constructive and professionally relevant contribution to the day, which he had long been looking forward to. The consultant said to Bob that it was very positive that he had opened up, and that it was important for the events of the day that everybody knew what the others were focused on, and that the things that were important were put on the table to make it easier to focus and be mentally present.

What sort of discourse forms the overall framework for this course of events? It is hardly a shared discourse, so let us rephrase the question to ask within which discourse the consultant's opening invitation might be understood. We might call this discourse *"let's get close"* – a discourse that is familiar in the Western culture, and which is related to the view of personal development in common-sense understandings and traditional individually focused psychology. It is based on two implicit assumptions. First, the assumption that mutual understanding requires us to reveal what is going on inside us, and second, that in order to be mentally present in an educational context and ready to learn we should first look inside and share what we find.

We surmise that Bob took the invitation, "Tell us where you're at right now" as part of a different discourse, perhaps a discourse which says that figures of authority know what they are doing, and that there is a purpose to what they do, even if it is not readily apparent. He follows the instruction and only later discovers the social impact of his reply: He becomes positioned as a person who needs compassion and help. He has no time to discover that his reply invites others into a position as empathetic helpers, which makes him part of a helping relationship; something that he had no desire for. The helping relationship develops in the situation the moment another participant willingly adopts the position of helper, placing Bob in a position that might be understood as feeble or weak within his personal story. He feels he has to object and turns to the consultant who initiated the course of events. The big task now facing Bob is to find a way in the subsequent events to position himself in a way that supports the identity story he wants for himself.

In communication terms, the instruction "Tell us where you're at right now" is not just an open and friendly phrase; it is a phrase that creates an ambiguous context with unclear boundaries for what constitutes a legitimate topic. It contains an invitation to position oneself as a private individual – not as a professionally competent and dedicated person in a workplace context. Thus, this seemingly "innocent" instruction contains a major moral challenge concerning how it contributes to positioning others.

POSITIONING THEORY

Positioning theory was developed by Bronwyn Davies, professor of education at University of Western Sydney, and Rom Harré, lecturer in the philosophy of science at Oxford University. Their new ideas were first presented in 1990 in the article *Positioning: The Discursive Production of Selves* (Davies & Harré, 1990). Since then, many others have taken up the ideas, and in 2003 they were the topic of a major interdisciplinary publication (Harré & Moghaddam, 2003). As we shall see, the authors are clearly inspired by Austin's and Wittgenstein's ideas.

We will now take a closer look at what characterizes *a position*. We will examine four key characteristics: Firstly, a position is a way of being defined in an ongoing conversation. Members of a Western culture or of a particular organization share thoughts and convictions about what it involves to hold certain positions, such as manager and employee or doctor and patient.

Secondly, positioning is a *relational* concept, i.e. one person steps into a position in relation to another person. A position cannot meaningfully be held in isolation. If someone stands in front of the bathroom mirror and declares him/herself the boss, the point is hardly to adopt a position in a discourse – unless the person is simply practicing using the word "boss" to be able to say it with conviction in front of the staff at a later time. Or unless the person is acting out an inner dialogue between, on the one hand, himself as a young boy who never thought he would become the boss, and, on the other hand, himself as an adult who is now formally appointed manager. However, in the ongoing communication of everyday life, the position as manager requires someone else to adopt the position as staff. In Story 5: *The Course Participant who was invited to share Private Information* we saw how the position as helper requires someone else to adopt the position as a person who needs help. Positions are complementary in the sense that they always exist in a reciprocal relationship. Thus, the way in which we position ourselves and others contributes to shaping our mutual relationships.

Thirdly, a position can be viewed as a *loosely defined set of moral obligations and entitlements* that include and define certain possibilities of action while excluding others: current and possibly temporary clusters of obligations and entitlements to think, act and speak in certain ways that seem obvious in the flow of everyday events (Harré & Moghaddam, 2003). Thus, we are not thinking of formally defined duties and rights that have been determined once and for all but of moral aspects of communication that may be fleeting. For example, the position as *newcomer* to an organization is not an unambiguous and objective description of the duration of a person's employment. In some organizations a person is positioned as newcomer for a few weeks; in other organizations the position may stick for months or even years. Being a newcomer expresses a position in relation to other people's position, complementary to *senior* or *experienced*. The position as newcomer implies certain moral obligations and entitlements. In many cases a newcomer is entitled to make missteps in relation to the informal norms in the organization but also an obligation to take a fresh and creative approach to things. A newcomer is allowed certain speech acts, such as asking about the order in the office breakfast arrangement, while other speech acts are not permitted – such as a sweeping criticism of procedures in the office.

Fourthly, in extension of the previous points, a position may be seen as *a negotiated place within a moral order.* The ongoing discourses contain invitations to adopt certain positions. It is one of the key ideas in social constructionism that people construct meaning by negotiating different versions of reality. The word *negotiation* may sound a little odd, since it may make us imagine a process that resembles an explicit negotiation at a negotiation table. That is not the way it is meant. Positioning theory explains the concept: *Negotiation* should be understood as the mutual process of influence where the participants in a discourse end up holding certain positions. Invitations to adopt certain positions are usually indirect, tucked away in language in subtle and unnoticeable ways. An attempt to place another person in the position of slacker may be so persistent in a given context that the person in question cannot see any means of escape. Objections would only serve to further cement the position.

Nevertheless, the theory underscores that the parties always have certain wriggle room. A doctor can hardly maintain the position of doctor if the man in the consultation room refuses to act as a patient, but insists on replacing a leaking water pipe that the secretary asked him to fix. Invitations to adopt positions have a temporary character that leaves room for the other person to accept, reject, reshape or object. Thus, there is room for personal choice within the culturally created repertoire of positions and speech acts.

The concept *position* is central to why an understanding of discourses is important to life in organizations – and therefore to managers, staff, and consultants. Harré and Moghaddam (2003) combine the concepts *position*, *story line* and *speech acts* in what they call the positioning triangle. They do not actually draw it, but here is our version:

Figure 4: The Positioning Triangle

STORY LINE
(THE NARRATIVE PLOT)

POSITIONS

SPEECH ACTS

The myriad events
of everyday life

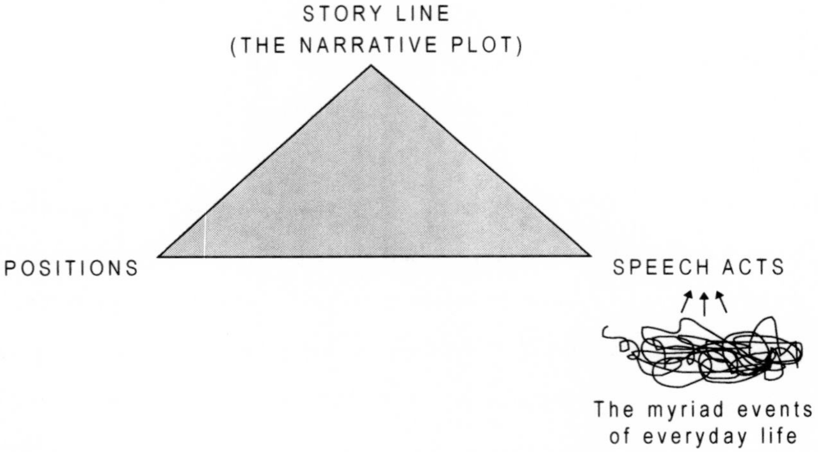

Story line corresponds to Pearce's *plot*, which we discussed in Chapter 3. Here, we will use the term *narrative plot*. The point of the model is that the three components interact and affect each other. Out of the myriad events of everyday life some events are co-created as speech acts, while others take a back seat. Speech acts can serve to enhance or undermine positions and the narrative plot. The narrative may include certain positions at the exclusion of others and thus facilitate certain speech acts over others.

We will now expand on this model and attempt to combine it with Pearce's key concepts of the contextual and implicative forces of communication. Figure 5 illustrates the contextual force.

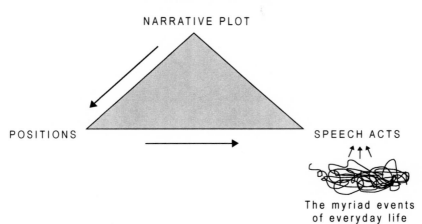

Figure 5: The Positioning Triangle
and Contextual Force

The arrows illustrate the contextual force that defines positions and restricts the scope of possible speech acts for the parties in a top-down motion. Let us use these concepts to shed new light on Story 2: *Friendly Concern or Sexual Harassment?*. As the title suggests, the story involved two competing narratives with very different plots. The story about sexual harassment became the dominant narrative and positioned the parties respectively as villain, victim, rescuer and spectator. A story with a plot about sexual harassment has a very strong contextual force. The positioning as villain denies the person the right to be recognized as a worthy work partner, while the position of victim gives the person the right to break off all communication with the villain. The positioning of rescuer obligates the person to protect the victim and to keep the villain away. A villain has the obligation to repent but has difficulty doing this face to face with the victim. To the extent that the parties accept these obligations the plot and everybody's positioning will be strengthened.

As we saw in this story, sexual harassment is a discourse where the contextual force is much stronger than the implicative force. None of the parties involved were able to come up with actions to change their positioning and the emplotment. We will later discuss the impact that a discourse on sexual harassment can have for the parties' mutual relationships.

In Figure 6 the arrows illustrate the implicative force. Positioning theory expands on both Austin's distinction between isolated utterances and actions (which carry no social meaning in themselves) and speech acts (in which social meaning has been co-created) and the use of the speech act concept in the CMM theory. The myriad isolated utterances and actions of everyday life may make entirely new contributions to the communication, which the actors manage to arrange into new speech acts that change the positions for those involved and mark the beginning of a new narrative.

Figure 6: The Positioning Triangle and Implicative Force

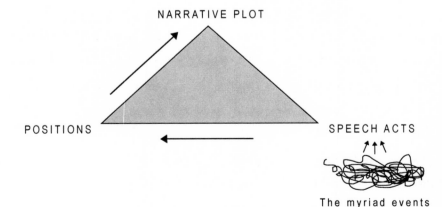

NARRATIVE PLOT

POSITIONS

SPEECH ACTS

The myriad events
of everyday life

We can now return to Story 5: *The Course Participant who was invited to share Private Information.* If Bob had accepted the position of a private individual who at a difficult time in his life needed comfort, support and help, he would have submitted to the contextual force of the activity and thus the narrative plot about the course participants who get together and help each other out. He did not. Through his act of criticizing the method he first took the position of critical participant toward the consultant in charge of the course and then probably other positions that better suited his preferred identity story. He put considerable effort into strengthening the implicative force in order to alter the narrative plot.

Positions, plots and speech acts are integral parts of discourses and can help organizational members understand what happens, and how it happens, in their everyday communication – and of course; how they can contribute to better communication for all parties involved.

Now, let us work with these concepts in order to unfold how well-known discourses shape life in organizations.

DISCOURSES OF DISRESPECTFUL RELATIONSHIPS

We will now examine four common discourses, each of which serves to position the participants as subject-object relationships, that is, as non-respectful relationships.

The Discourse on Change Management

In Western cultures it is considered indisputable that reality changes at a rapidly accelerating rate, and that change management is among any leader's most important skills. The discourse on change management is inescapable.

Change management has been on the agenda for decades. There is a huge literature on change management (see, for example, Kanter, 1996 and Kotter, 1997).

This discourse makes three positions available. There is the position as change *sponsors*, which is defined as persons with formal authority (the board of directors, political decision-makers, top management), the position as *change agents* (mid-level management and consultants) and the position as *affected* (employees). Change sponsors and change agents are sometimes the same. In most literature on change management the main focus is on change agents and the affected. A change agent is the subject who has to know something about the object, for example about the employees' attitudes to change, their worries and likely resistance to change. The subject's dominant position is also illustrated linguistically with the term change agent, which clearly refers to the subject's active position and agency, while the terminology is ambiguous where the object is concerned. Here we have only the somewhat cumbersome term the affected. The term suggests the object's passive role: The employees are affected by outside changes. Hosking (2006) emphasizes that many traditional assumptions about change invite a subject-object relationship.

In the prevailing version of change management, change is seen as the result of the execution of a planned process, where the organization is moved from one stable state to a new stable state. Once the sponsors have made the general decisions, it is up to the change agents to manage the process based on an empirically founded, rational analysis, precise knowledge about the original position and a clear vision of the end-goal. Change is thus seen as an extraordinary phase bridging two stable periods. In his or her role as change agent the manager is expected to possess privileged knowledge in relation to the employees – about the organization's original position and the end-goal. Thus, the manager should aim to *control* the change process and steer the organizational unit through the transition as quickly and efficiently as possible. As a subject, the change agent should both know something about the object and affect it. If this subject-object relationship fails to develop harmoniously – as it often does – the disharmony is explained with reference to qualities in the manager, who "is" not charismatic enough, or the employee, who "is" not sufficiently open to change. In many cases, the manager will act as the knowing subject who is able to diagnose the employee as an object: "He/she is resisting change."

In this discourse on change management managers and employees are unnoticeably enrolled in their positions as change agents and affected. The positioning is strongly reliant on the persons' formal job titles and thus seems self-evident. In case of a merger or a restructuring, middle managers hold the position as change agents, which equips the individual middle manager with certain moral obligations and entitlements. The middle manager is entitled to receive relevant and adequate information from the sponsors about the general decisions and obligated to convey this information in ways that are adapted to the various staff groups based on the manager's particular knowledge of these groups. The change agent is rarely entitled to criticize the sponsors' decisions or demand that they are revoked. However, the change agent does have the obligation to make sure that the staff will not only accept the change but embrace it. In the case of any resistance to the change, it is up to the change agent to apply appropriate methods to alter the mood, including information, explanation, lecturing, persuasion or whatever the situation calls for.

Those affected have the right to ask questions about the consequences of the change process but usually not about the necessity of change. Questioning whether a planned merger is a good idea at all is usually seen as verging on the inappropriate. Whether or not the affected are happy about the change, they are obligated to adapt. If one of them persists in questioning the sponsors' decisions the person has an obligation to determine whether he or she is going to go along with the process or look for another job.

Thus, the prevailing discourse on change management offers a very limited number of positions, which are characterized by various obligations and entitlements. Most of the organizational members – the employees – are positioned as affected – a position that may well become a victim position. Victims are rarely expected to make energetic, creative or constructive contributions. Victims flee or keep a low profile until the danger has passed; an example of the self-fulfilling power of discourses.

The Discourse on Individual Dysfunction, Diagnosis and Treatment

We will now look at another familiar discourse in Western culture: that of individual dysfunction, diagnosis and treatment. In recent decades, this discourse has increasingly invaded our work life and our understanding of what goes on in organizations. The range of what is commonly perceived as being *dysfunctional* in organizational members has gradually expanded. If a manager or a staff member is not performing well, the explanation might be that there is something wrong with the person. He or she may be sick, long-term sick, suffering from stress, in a crisis, a victim of bullying, a victim of sexual harassment, a victim of violence, a victim of a destructive boss, an alcoholic, troubled by a divorce or undergoing an existential mid-life crisis – to mention but a few examples.

Rose (1999) has offered an important culture-critical analysis of the growing tendency to introduce health perspectives and therapy into all areas of life. In this discourse, managers should have enhanced knowledge about the possible individual dysfunctions that might affect other organizational members. This hands the manager a challenging task: He or she should be able to diagnose, for example, whether a staff member is suffering from stress, burnout or is undergoing a crisis. All three "conditions" have emerged within recent decades.

Burnout is commonly perceived as a condition that may affect people in jobs that revolve around helping others and which require a particularly high degree of personal contact, care, empathy and understanding. The problem was identified in the United States in the 1970s and was labeled the *burnout syndrome* – a catch phrase for a wide range of psychosomatic symptoms that were particularly common among persons in socially demanding jobs such as social workers, nurses, police officers, teachers, prison staff, etc. In Denmark the issue has been on the agenda since the late 1980s. Burnout is understood as a state of emotional fatigue where the affected person develops an impersonal view of the recipients of his or her services and a negative appraisal of his or her own contributions.

The crisis concept stems from clinical psychology where it is applied to a wide range of life crises stemming from divorce, bereavement, traumatic accidents, and chronic disease. The idea that managers need to consider the staff members' life crises is relatively new and was introduced in an organizational context in connection with the idea that a company's HR policy should address *the whole person*. Some trade unions have embraced this point of view and thus recommend that crisis intervention be included as a benefit in collective agreements.

The overall discourse on dysfunction in relation to work life contains a variety of discourses about what might be wrong with organizational members. In the following we will use bullying as an example of a discourse that is familiar both in the Western culture and in organizational cultures and which generates narratives that lock all the involved parties into certain positions.

In most Danish and international research literature, bullying is defined as something that occurs when one or more individuals repeatedly and over an extended period is/are exposed to negative and aggressive acts by one or more individuals, and where it is difficult for the victim(s) to defend themselves.

In our view of bullying as a cultural discourse the model introduced previously becomes illustrative and relevant:

Figure 7: The Cultural Discourse on Bullying

SPECIFIC STORY
ABOUT BULLYING

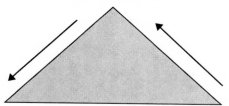

POSITIONS
- Presumed bully
- Bully
- Victim of bullying
- Passive witness
- Witness

THE BULLY'S ACTIONS, e.g.:
- Hurtful comments
- Criticism of the victim's private life
- Slander
- Exclusion from community
- Scolding
- Ridicule
- Offensive phone calls
- Unpleasant teasing
- Denigration due to sex or age

The cultural discourse on bullying makes some 5-6 positions available to the persons involved in the discourse. The position labels shown in Figure 7 appear in many manuals about anti-bullying initiatives in the workplace. Some of these manuals contain an additional position for the manager who abandons his or her position as a passive witness and adopts a new position as *rescuer*. It is interesting to note that all the positions – except the position of rescuer – are negatively charged.

Once the bullying discourse has been initiated the narrative characterizing the given organizational culture places certain persons into the various positions. What moral obligations and entitlements do the positions imply? A positioning as victim takes away the person's entitlement and obligation to appear as a co-responsible contributor. A victim deserves our pity. A victim is without fault. A victim is weak; too weak to handle his or her job. In return, the victim is entitled to expect protection from others and assistance in sanctions against the bully. As illustrated in Story 2: *Friendly Concern or Sexual Harassment?* Hank was positioned as the villain by a coworker who – with her manager's acceptance – had positioned herself as the victim. That denied Hank the right to talk to the victim, and he was excluded from his project team. In the earlier discussion of this story we illustrated how powerful this discourse is, and how all the persons involved were locked into positions that made it extremely difficult to reshape the relationships. Here it is difficult for the persons involved to escape the story's contextual force.

Figure 7 also includes examples of acts that are defined as bullying behavior in the bullying discourse. This notion rests on the idea that a single utterance or action is meaningful in itself. That is the logic that is illustrated in Figure 7, as if a singular act could be defined, for example, as "a hurtful comment". As we discussed in Chapter 3, the CMM theory offers a completely different understanding of events: *Utterances and actions only take on meaning as part of a larger whole.* Whether a comment is hurtful or not depends on the context, relationship, and previous and subsequent events. Thus, the interesting issue to explore in relation to bullying is how the involved organizational members arrange some of the myriad utterances and actions of everyday life into speech acts that are labeled as bullying (at the exclusion of other utterances and actions). How does a story about bullying even develop? As we saw in Story 2: *Friendly Concern or Sexual*

Harassment? multiple actors were involved in giving prevalence to the story about sexual harassment.

Thus, from a social constructionist perspective Figure 7 is misleading, and a more adequate depiction would be the one below (Figure 8). The interesting part is to explore how events from the myriad of events in everyday work life become co-created as "bullying".

Figure 8: The Making of a Story about Bullying

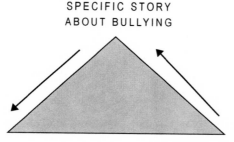

SPECIFIC STORY
ABOUT BULLYING

POSITIONS:
Presumed bully
Bully
Victim of bullying
Passive witness
Witness

SPEECH ACTS, e.g.:
Ridicule,
Denigration of gender/age,
Slander

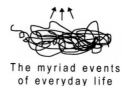

The myriad events
of everyday life

Placing persons into the available positions in a bullying discourse not only shapes their mutual relationships, it also equips them with a certain identity. In our common-sense understanding the victim is a person who is entitled to care, the bully is an unpleasant person, and the passive witness is a wimp.

So how do we counter bullying from the perspective of a common-sense understanding or traditional anti-bullying literature with its roots in realism? Here we may turn again to the manuals mentioned earlier. They contain advice both for preventing the problem and for handling bullying and sexual harassment in the workplace once it occurs. A manual from a trade union offers some "good advice" for the victim of bullying who is advised first of all to talk to close friends, family or trusted colleagues. Next, the manual emphasizes that victims of bullying should not let the problems dominate their lives, and that they should find places they can "call sanctuary", keep their spirits up (when things are bad, one should try to think of all the good things in life), stay healthy (avoiding the use of sedatives or anti-anxiety medicine), talk to a professional who can offer an outside perspective (someone from the union is recommended), contact the workplace safety representative – and prepare to have a meeting with management.

As indicated, there is no advice for the victim to contact the bully. The interesting aspect of the suggestions mentioned here is that they perpetuate the victimization of the person – albeit unintended. There is no advice about how to set boundaries in relation to the bully, reshape the context, act in ways that counteract the arrangement of actions into the speech act of bullying, etc. – possibilities for action that we addressed in Chapter 3 in the section on social responsibility. In the CMM theory it is an important point that everybody involved in a story can help change it, for example, by contributing to more respectful speech acts and by positioning oneself and others in new ways, thus enhancing the implicative force to make room for new and more positive positions.

In the discourse on dysfunction in the workplace managers are increasingly required to learn to diagnose. They should know something about the phenomena of burnout and stress and the harmful health effects of bullying and sexual harassment, including possible early symptoms, how the "condition" might develop, and how they can intervene most effectively. The spread of the discourse on individual dysfunction in the workplace increasingly serves to place managers and staff into subject-object relationships.

The diagnostic approach is about counting incidents, assessing the scope of the problem and positioning specific individuals into negatively loaded plot positions. In recent decades the underlying focus on problems and deficiencies has been built into many HR tools such as employee satisfaction studies, workplace climate surveys, management performance assessments, etc. where employees are asked questions that aim to uncover their stress levels (for example "Do you have trouble sleeping at night?"), and whether they have been exposed to bullying, sexual harassment or violence. These HR tools create subject-object relationships and define the involved organization members' moral obligations and entitlements in restricting ways.

The Discourse on Documentation and Evaluation

We have looked at some familiar discourses that place the organizational participants in debilitating subject-object relationships. The discourse on documentation and evaluation has a different character than those previously discussed, as it does not primarily consist of face-to-face communication, but is structured by systems, policies and work procedures that are typically imposed on the organization either from the outside (in the form of legislation) or from above (in the form of requirements from higher levels within the larger organization).

This discourse exists in a variety of forms both in the public and the private sector. Since the 1990s the Danish public sector has seen an incorporation of market terms and mechanisms in the form of New Public Management, and management based on goals and outcomes has gained increasing prominence. For example, the directors of municipal residential facilities for persons with mental illness are required to produce annual reports, corporate plans and a large number of ad hoc reports on request from the municipal authority. Managers in these facilities must ensure careful and regular documentation for use in connection with the many types of inspections including health and safety inspections, educational audits from the municipal authorities, environmental inspections, fire safety inspections, financial audits, etc. Staff performance and development reviews must be carried out annually to draw up development plans for the individual employee, and the list of mandatory plans further include education and development plans for the individual resident, emergency plans, crisis plans, plans to prevent violence, action plans to reduce sick leave, etc., etc.

Pre-school teachers are required to draw up development plans, annual plans, individualized education plans, and plans to improve the pre-school environment for the children. Domestic service for senior citizens is already subject to detailed minute-by-minute calculations of the time allotted for individual activities, and domestic service workers are required to provide detailed documentation for their work. School teachers are required to draw up individualized education plans, and social workers have to record every single step that a recipient of unemployment benefits has taken to find work.

Good results are rewarded publicly with happy smileys or good ratings. Organizations with mediocre results are punished in public with frowning smileys or low ratings. The national government has introduced a smiley system to rate hygiene and food safety procedures in the food and restaurant industry and is considering introducing it as a quality rating for hospitals.

Many public and private companies require their employees to log how many minutes and hours they spend on various tasks on a daily basis. In public organizations the goal is to provide information for management as a basis for planning tasks and allocate man-hours; in private companies it is mainly used for project planning and invoicing. As an employee told us recently, "*Even though there are many activity categories, interestingly, there's no category for the registration task itself. If I were to do this completely by the book, I would have to spend 10-12 minutes a day or about an hour every week. Since that one hour can't be registered anywhere, does that mean I'm supposed to work 38 hours a week to document that I work 37?*" This story is interesting for two reasons. Firstly, it illustrates a personal dilemma as a consequence of what might be called a system error. It seems illogical to have to log everything except the time spent logging. Secondly, it invites concerns on the level of society as a whole: Wonder how many man-hours are spent documenting, reporting and planning? In the discourse of documentation and evaluation that would seem to be an obvious question. However, we have not managed to find a single study to bring us closer to an answer.

The explicit rationale for the extensive use of documentation, control measures, evaluations and certification is that these initiatives promote the motivation to achieve high performance and insure effective use of funds. Furthermore, the initiatives aim to enable comparisons, which are supposed to promote competition and make it possible to impose the necessary consequences on the ones that perform inadequately.

Management appraisals are an illustrative case in point. Most large and medium-sized companies use management appraisals. These are often in the form of a so-called 360-degree appraisal (also called feedback, analysis, review or evaluation), where the manager appraises him/herself and is also appraised by employees, colleagues, supervisors and possibly by clients or external partners. The parameters are often generic, which means that the providers of the 360-degree instrument have looked to theory or experience to articulate a series of topics that are assumed to be of general relevance for management performance in any organization. These typically relate to general topics such as communication, cooperation, planning and results. For each topic, the appraisal involves a series of utterances which respondents then use to assess the person on a scale, for example on a scale from 1 through 10. Once all replies are in, the outcome is summarized in graphs and diagrams that state average scores, standard deviations, etc. These quantitative findings are then typically discussed in a meeting between the manager and an external or internal consultant. A study by the Danish Centre for Leadership found that manager appraisals are mainly practiced with the declared purpose of enhancing the manager's self-insight and thus facilitate his or her development process (Danish Centre for Leadership, 2006). To achieve this, evaluation responses are kept anonymous to ensure that the full "truth" comes out. There is considerable emphasis on confronting managers with any differences between their own and others' appraisal of them and on developing action plans and follow-up plans. When management appraisals are used systematically, the appraisal is repeated once a year to hold the individual manager to his or her development plans and check up on the degree of improvement.

360-degree management appraisals are recommended by many experts in the field of human resources. For example, the Danish Professor Henrik Holt Larsen of the Copenhagen Business School writes, *"In terms of validity, it strengthens the method that any inaccuracies or actually flawed appraisals from any one source are 'washed out' or 'diluted' because they are combined with appraisals from other sources (…) The main drawbacks are the considerable practical work effort the method requires and the discomfort that some stakeholders might feel in having to do the appraisal"* (Larsen, 2006, p. 303; translated for this edition).

The method clearly falls within the linear understanding and relies on certain implicit assumptions about personal appraisals and development. The first assumption is that if only we amass a sufficiently large body of data we will wind up with a correct impression of the person under appraisal. The second assumption is that the flawed appraisals by a few respondents will be balanced out by the more correct appraisals of the majority. The third assumption is that feedback about who a manager "really is" will form a sound basis for personal development.

Although the stated purpose is usually the individual manager's personal development, many companies find management appraisals useful in a range of other applications. The rationale is that once all these ratings have been produced one ought to make the most of them, for the sake of efficiency. In our consultancy work we have encountered many alternative applications that go beyond what was agreed, for example the use of management appraisals as a basis for decisions about bonuses, promotions, and dismissals.

Another popular application is benchmarking against other companies: If the managers of one company score an average of 6.2 on communication on a ten-point scale, how does that compare to other companies? Do our managers score lower, the same or higher on communication than managers from other companies? These comparisons are assumed to indicate where improvement efforts are most needed.

Let us apply the concept of positioning in relation to the discourse on documentation and evaluation. How are managers and employees positioned in relation to each other and in relation to the authorities?

Government control, that is, control which the organizational members perceive as external, is likely to be perceived as distrust by both employees and managers. Essentially, they are under suspicion of not doing their jobs well enough: suspected of sloppiness, errors, ignorance, irresponsibility, indifference and perhaps even inhumanity. They are constantly under suspicion. For example, institutions often provide careful reports without receiving any sort of feedback on whether they did well enough. If an inspection visit or a review "failed to find anything" the thinking is that maybe the measures were too lax. If an inspection visit did find something reprehensible, it is proof of the need for inspections, which should therefore be carried out even more frequently to make sure that managers and employees cannot continue to act reprehensibly. The contextual force of this discourse is very powerful and shapes subject-object relationships between government authorities and heads of institutions.

The heads of institutions find themselves in a particularly complex situation as they are both under suspicion and required to check on their employees; the employees in turn are both under suspicion of not doing their jobs well enough and for possibly failing to document and report truthfully. This creates subject-object relationships between manager and employees.

This discourse also has powerful consequences for the communication that is promoted within the organization. Registration and documentation requires a breakdown into elements that can be counted, rated and measured and then subjected to statistical analysis. This invites managers and employees to think in a linear mode and to focus on problems and deficiencies. The focus is directed at quantitative information about the past, written information and one-way communication. Again, management appraisals offer an illustrative example: In the efforts to achieve a comprehensive impression of the individual manager's managerial skills the appraisal collects anonymous replies based on the assumption that people only tell the truth when they cannot be held accountable. These appraisals are then added up, and average scores are calculated. Based on these average scores the manager is supposed to know what to do to improve. However, the anonymity prevents any subsequent dialogue between manager and employees, a point that we will revisit in Chapter 7. Quite contrary to intentions, any direct contact is hampered, and the potential for management development is diminished. As a result of the methods used in the discourse on documentation and evaluation, both managers and employees have to work hard to change their action and thought patterns away from the ones discussed above and create contexts in which dialogue is possible: Contexts in which it is possible to learn about the complex connections and interactions among organizational members and among employees and their clients, residents, customers, patients etc., to whom they want to deliver the best possible service. Thus, in spite of the very best intentions, the discourse on documentation and evaluation risks becoming an obstacle to learning, quality improvement, creativity, and development.

This discourse is associated with a certain degree of magical thinking and excessive faith in numbers. It is taken for granted that numerical changes reflect changes over time, for example with regard to average waiting time for diagnosis in hospitals, number of complaints, cases handled per month or an improvement from 3.5 to 4.0 in a question about satisfaction in a workplace climate survey. This assumption rests firstly on the conviction that the same number two years in a row reflects the same qualitative situation, and that numerical changes reflect a corresponding change in reality. Comparing numbers over time is based on the assumption that all other things are equal, that is, unchanged. Take the example of a workplace climate survey. In 2005 the average assessment of a question about a particular manager's ability to motivate his employees was 3.1 on a five-point scale. In 2006 the average was 2.1. It is overwhelmingly likely that this change will be interpreted as a step backward for the manager, reflecting a drop in employee satisfaction. The manager will be facing a reprimand. But all other things are *not* equal. Perhaps in the intervening year the employees have become much happier with their work, so they expect more of their manager. Perhaps there have been replacements among the staff; the manager may have been less physically present in the department, and so on. As we discussed in Chapter 3 words and sentences have no meaning in themselves, only in context. If the questions change meaning over time the scores are not comparable.

Secondly, the faith in numbers and the magical thinking are associated with the conviction that once something has been committed to paper it has become more real and more effective. Consequently, changes in the numerical values in management appraisals, workplace climate surveys etc. can be used to reward or hold those responsible accountable. Thus, records, documentation, plans, appraisals and control measures easily invite moralizing, condemnation, blame games and sanctions – phenomena that do *not* facilitate learning and development.

As far as we can tell, the discourse on documentation and evaluation appears to be losing ground in the public sector. There is growing criticism in the public debate that questions the legitimacy of the documentation requirements. The requirements may be based on legislation, but they are increasingly referred to as mere paper shuffling and red tape. Once the legitimacy is widely questioned, civil disobedience becomes a possibility. From our consultancy work we are familiar with several examples of collective as well as individual forms of protest and civil disobedience. For example, some managers check off staff performance, development reviews and management appraisals on the list of carried out tasks simply to satisfy the HR department and get them off their back, even if these activities have not in fact taken place.

The discourse on documentation and evaluation not only implies a negative view of management and staff, it also rests on essential assumptions about learning and development, which we will discuss in the following chapter. For now, we will simply conclude that the positioning imposed by this discourse on managers and employees is not conducive to well-executed services and quality improvements in the workplace. It also does nothing to facilitate dialogue and mutual appreciation.

NEGATIVE EFFECTS OF THE THREE DISCOURSES

In this chapter we have discussed how certain familiar and culturally embedded discourses position organizational actors and shape their mutual relationships in certain ways. Furthermore, the participation in discourses invites certain forms of communication. The discourses on change management, on individual dysfunction and on documentation and evaluation are discourses that shape subject-object relationships. Positioning within a subject-object relationship defines certain forms of communication as appropriate and excludes others. The key point here is that a subject-object relationship minimizes dialogue and mutual respect.

Narratives about villains evoke the positioning of victims – and vice versa. We have demonstrated how both the professional literature and the popular literature abound with labels for villains. The villain may be a bully, the perpetrator of sexual harassment or abuse, mean, vicious, destructive, callous, a psychopath, etc. A position as villain is something that is assigned or imposed by others, while it is extremely rare that an organizational member perceives him/herself as a villain. When the positioning is "successful", that is, when a majority or a loud or otherwise strong minority has managed to position a particular person as a villain, the villain's denial of being a villain is simply seen to confirm this moral character.

When members of an organization manage to cast a particular person in a position as, say, a bully or a psychopath, events take a certain turn with moral consequences.

Firstly, someone who is positioned as a villain is denied a voice and thus the opportunity to tell his or her side of the story and his or her version of reality. The value of the person's life experience is refuted. The labeling can be extremely effective – in fact more effective than if the person had been brought up on criminal charges. In a court of law the accused would have had the right to speak and the right to a defense counsel. In organizational discourses about bullying or about the destructive boss there is no defense counsel. An organizational member can be labeled without even knowing it and without being heard.

Secondly, a person in a victim position is relieved of the obligation to engage in dialogue. The obligation to speak to and take an interest in others is one of the most important moral obligations in an organization. Employees are obligated to speak with their manager, and vice versa. Coworkers in a work team are obligated to talk to each other. Differences in sex, age, ethnic background, etc. do not relieve organizational members from the obligation to speak to each other. In most organizational cultures, likes and dislikes are not seen as a legitimate basis for making individual decisions about whom to talk to and whom to ignore. This obligation goes both ways: One is obligated both to speak and to listen. As we discussed in Chapter 4, intricate cultural norms determine how this obligation is to be acted upon (for example with regard to turn-taking in a conversation). In discourses about bullying and the destructive boss, the victim is not only entitled to break off his or her own communication with the villain, but also to attempt to isolate the villain from communication with others.

Thirdly, discourses about bullying and sexual harassment cultivate fear and suspicion. Literature on these issues often includes advice to the victim on what to do: Avoid all contact with the offender, gather evidence, try to catch the offender red-handed, and warn colleagues against the offender. The main message is that the victim is powerless and in danger, that it is important to take one´s fear seriously, and keep a safe distance from the offender. This literature is deeply rooted in common-sense linear causality and its tendency to blame others and ignore our own shared responsibility for events that take place.

Fourthly, it is clear that a subject-object relationship implies power – the power to define the object, that is, to state how this person *really is*. The subject has the right to make statements about the object, while the object has no right to make statements about the subject or about him/herself. The object can either accept the accusation or try to defend him/herself but has very limited chances of changing the narrative plot.

REFLECTIONS

We can now conclude that discourses that generate subject-object relationships do not help shape a better social world. That applies also to research and studies on organizations that spring from these discourses. Why is that? Surely, the purpose of studying bullying must be to end it? And surely, workplace climate surveys, satisfaction surveys and management appraisals are carried out with the purpose of improving conditions for managers and employees? There is no doubt about the good intentions. But if we link this aspiration with Pearce's concepts of spectator knowledge and participatory knowledge we arrive at an interesting question: How do the researchers and surveyors imagine that it is possible to move from spectator knowledge about what *not* to do to participatory knowledge about what we *can* do?

Both studies and surveys of problems and dysfunction in the workplace rest on a set of assumptions about the course of problem-solving, change and development:

1. Research and studies contribute an adequate and objective description of a pre-existing reality.
2. Research and studies can be carried out without affecting the social reality.

3. Knowledge about the severity, scope and extent of the problem (expressed in percentages) has a strong motivating force.

4. Research and studies should be based on unambiguous definitions and lead to general regularities that can be applied to any and all organizations.

5. When the causes of the problems are uncovered the persons involved will be able to prevent and address them.

From a social constructionist perspective these assumptions are not helpful. Instead we need respectful methods that are capable of generating participatory knowledge.

We have searched the literature on bullying in vain for ethical reflections on the effects of studying bullying. Given the assumption that it is possible to gather data without affecting reality, it is understandable that these ethical reflections are absent. In 2006 the Danish government allocated several million Danish kroner to do research into bullying in the workplace. We fear that this research might give the bullying discourse an even more prominent place on the agenda in organizations and cause even more managers and employees to be positioned as bullies, victims and witnesses – with everyone as losers.

How, then, can we create useful insight into social worlds in morally responsible ways? Our main focus is on the obligation to *listen discursively* to what others are saying, to listen to conversations as narratives, and to explore our own and other people's underlying assumptions about how events are arranged into narrative plots. Discursive listening involves a great responsibility for paying attention to the way in which we position ourselves and others as well as a responsibility to explore whether the ongoing positioning facilitates the construction of a better social world. Discursive listening is the first step in an effort to deconstruct harmful discourses in an organization and accept the shared responsibility for helping to construct alternative discourses and narratives that shape mutually respectful relationships and respectful communication.

To take the next steps we must first explore how we can shape subject-subject relationships, practice the obligation to engage in dialogue, and help generate participatory knowledge that is helpful for everybody involved. This effort involves several essential concepts — especially the concept of appreciation, which is the topic of the next chapter.

CHAPTER 6

INQUIRY AND APPRECIATION OF VALUE TO THE WORK COMMUNITY

We will now explore how mutually respectful relationships are created in organizations. In the previous chapter we saw how various versions of subject-object relationships are anchored in certain discourses. A discourse makes certain positions available while excluding many others. The way in which communication is shaped places the involved persons in these positions, which produces relations of a certain nature. That brings us to the crucial point that changing subject-object relationships requires changing the dominant discourse or perhaps creating an entirely different discourse. For example, staging an anti-bullying effort in an organization to prevent people from being positioned as victims of bullying, bullies or passive witnesses requires changing the discourse and the forms of communication that make these positions available.

To generate discourses that enable mutually respectful relationships we need some additional concepts, particularly the concepts of *inquiry, shared learning* and *appreciation.* Appreciative Inquiry[1] is one of the more recent and promising approaches to using language and communication to promote

1 For a thorough introduction and overview of Appreciative Inquiry, see Barrett, F. & Fry, R, Appreciative Inquiry: A Positive Approach to Building Cooperative Capacity. (Taos Institute Publiciations, 2005).

shared learning as well as strengthening mutual relationships. Appreciative Inquiry involves two essential components: appreciation and inquiry. In this chapter we will examine how each of these components contributes to a constructive process. First, we turn to John Dewey and Axel Honneth. John Dewey made an important contribution with the concept of *inquiry*. Axel Honneth gave the concept of recognition or appreciation a key place in his writings. Both writers focus on the ethical aspects of ongoing communication in everyday life.

We will use the work of these two authors to shed new light on Appreciative Inquiry, which is a philosophy, a theory and a practice that is seeing increasing use in efforts to enhance the conditions for shared learning and development in organizations.

INQUIRY AS EXPERIENTIAL LEARNING: JOHN DEWEY

John Dewey (1859-1952) was an American philosopher, psychologist and educator. Dewey was a very prolific writer and produced many works that have remained important sources of inspiration to this day. In 1884 Dewey took a Ph.D. with a dissertation on Kantian psychology. Dewey's next project was a basic textbook on psychology, which was published in 1887. This book was based on Hegel's ideas about man as a being that needs others' appreciation in order to develop self-consciousness. Dewey was first employed as a teacher of philosophy at the University of Michigan and from 1894 as a professor at the University of Chicago, where he and his wife established a school with a very experimental educational approach: the *laboratory school*. The idea for the school stemmed from Dewey's criticism of the emphasis on theoretical knowledge in the school system and the students' passive reception of this knowledge. Instead, the laboratory school was organized as a cooperative community where the students' learning was anchored in practical activities and cooperation on concrete problem-solving.

Alongside the psychologist William James, John Dewey is considered one of the most important writers in the school of *pragmatism*. Pragmatism can be seen as an epistemology which assumes that ideas are tools that people use to manage the world they live in. Dewey did not distinguish between theory and practice but saw theory as another form of practice.

Pragmatism has been an important source of inspiration for the development of social constructionism and, as part of this, the CMM theory, which we described in Chapter 3. At the same time, Dewey must be considered a realist and lived long before the labeling of a new paradigm as social constructionism. Nevertheless, some of his ideas have served as springboards for social constructionist thinkers. In the following, we will highlight some of these ideas.

Dewey's thinking was based on the notion that the world is changing and impermanent, and that everything is in constant flux. He was not focused on objects, but on processes. Thus, in the preface to *Experience and Nature*, he writes, *"It is then shown that the foundation for value and the striving to realize it is found in nature, because when nature is viewed as consisting of events rather than substances, it is characterized by histories, that is, by continuity of change proceeding from beginnings to endings"* (Dewey, originally 1925, this edition 1958, pp. xi-xii). In this book, Dewey uses an example that clouds and mountains can be understood as events. At first glance, it is easy to view cloud formations as fleeting processes, always in motion and rapidly changing shape and color. However, Dewey says, the only difference between clouds and mountains is a difference in time frame. Mountains too are in motion and change color and shape. The changes simply take longer. That implies the interesting notion that what we perceive as things might instead be seen as frozen snapshots of processes unfolding over time. Dewey did not attribute any positive value per se to the processual and changeable character of reality, he simply noted it as a basic condition that poses a challenge to man. People's response to this basic condition varies historically and across cultures. Here, Dewey criticizes the widespread tendency to deny the basic changeability and developmental nature of reality: *"Our magical safeguard against the uncertain character of the world is to deny the existence of chance, to mumble universal and necessary law, the ubiquity of cause and effect, the uniformity of nature, universal progress, and the inherent rationality of the universe"* (Dewey, 1925, p. 44). Dewey further explains that we use science to achieve power in the form of predictability and control, believing that we can achieve protection from the risks of the world. However, we cannot eliminate the arbitrary character of the world. At best, we can hope to obscure the fact.

Dewey wrote this in 1925. The points might as well have been made today in a comment to contemporary research into problems in organizations and the growing use of studies aiming to control, manage and increase predictability (see Chapter 5). In the public debate, the intrepid reporter who has identified a problem almost invariably asks, *"So, how are you going to make sure that this never happens again?"* In Dewey's paradigm we would say the uncertainty and unpredictability of events in organizations is simply a basic condition. It would be an illusion to think that additional knowledge can put an end to uncertainty and unpredictability. However, additional knowledge could be used to help us endure and deal with uncertainty and unpredictability. What sort of knowledge would be required to achieve this is a point we will get back to later.

This desire to eliminate uncertainty is the topic of a subsequent book: *The Quest for Certainty* (Dewey, 1929). Here, Dewey first describes two different responses springing from the realization that the world is not only changing and unpredictable but also dangerous. One response is to try to reconcile with the powers that govern one's fate. Throughout history this response has been expressed in a multitude of ways including magic, ritual sacrifice and self-discipline, where the efforts are directed at working with oneself and one's ideas and emotions in order to reconcile with fate. This line of thinking is reflected in the prevailing contemporary discourse on personal development – a discourse that saddles the individual with the obligation to work on their personal growth and development.

The second response would be to try to change the world through actions that shape our living conditions, which is the objective of pragmatism. This approach – says Dewey – has been disparaged historically, as philosophers have instead celebrated methods aimed at changing personal ideas (Dewey, 1929). How is this endeavor approached? To answer this question we must first examine some of the consequences of viewing reality in terms of either objects or processes.

Viewing reality as a collection of objects encourages a view where they are seen as disparate entities with stable characteristics that affect each other like billiard balls bouncing off each other, changing paths without affecting each other's inherent properties. Dewey calls this *interaction*.

If instead we view reality as events we have to replace the concept of *objects* with *processes*. Events are processes characterized by complexity, temporality and transaction. *Complexity* refers to the necessity of understanding entities in their varying interactions with the environment. It is an illusion to believe that we can select an entity and study it in isolation from other entities. Thus, Dewey would object to the idea that it is possible to identify a manager's personality as an object that can be described in itself, separate from a variable environment. *Temporality* means that events must always be seen in a temporal context. This idea is reflected in social constructionism, for example in the notion that attributing meaning to an event depends on the temporal perspective from which it is viewed. It makes a difference whether an event is viewed in the perspective of the past, the present or the future. We discuss this point about the *perspective of time* as a context marker for events in a previous publication (Haslebo, 2004). The third characteristic of events is *transaction*, which characterizes the phenomenon that components of events have a mutual effect on each other and are themselves changed in the process. While the notion of interacting objects encourages us to look for causes in underlying factors, that is, object properties, the notion of processes encourages an interest in describing the patterns of the mutual influences without looking for underlying causes.

The concept of transaction is reflected in the CMM model's ideas about mutual influence in communication that is illustrated in the conversational triplet: An utterance can change meaning both prospectively and retroactively (see Chapter 3). Utterances are ambiguous and have no meaning in themselves; instead they are part of events that change meaning over time. It is a key concept for Dewey that development is driven by events in transaction

– not by underlying causal forces. Dewey, who was very interested in the ongoing discussions in contemporary physics, drew inspiration from Einstein's theory of relativity and Niels Bohr's thinking on physics. In extension of Einstein's theory Dewey did not view time, space and movement as natural properties but as relational phenomena that could be described in a variety of ways depending on the observer. Dewey awards the concept of transaction a key role in all science. Thus, he criticizes the prevailing scientific thinking, which he calls a *spectator approach* to science. The spectator approach is based, firstly, on the assumption that it is possible to keep the selected subject areas constant while the observation takes place, and secondly, that scientists or observers can apply their methods without affecting the subject area. If we compare this understanding with our discussion in Chapter 5, for example in relation to studies of bullying, we note that these studies are based on a spectator approach to generating information. However, the big question is whether they are capable of generating information that can become knowledge in Dewey's use of the word: *usage in practice*. Can spectator knowledge be used to change events in practice? Hardly. Dewey claims that the spectator theory on knowledge not only misses the mark but also has some very unfortunate social consequences as it creates a divide between "those who know" and "those who do not know". This approach to scientific thinking is associated with the generation of relationships that are not mutually respectful, which Hosking calls subject-object relationships (Hosking, 2006). Similarly, we now see the inspiration from Dewey in Pearce's distinction between spectator knowledge and participatory knowledge (Pearce, 2007b).

Isolated bits of information do not make sense in themselves and cannot automatically be transmuted into useful knowledge. It takes much more than that, and Dewey has a suggestion – which we will now review.

Experience and Participatory Knowledge

Dewey viewed science as a practice that involves human *action*. To know something about reality we must intervene in reality in ways that are guided by practical reason and then study the effects of these interventions. Experience includes the entire process of acting and then testing how our actions affect reality and ourselves. Experience is a *transactional* process where meaning is created in a specific social context. Thus, Dewey did not perceive experience as an individual phenomenon, that is, as something that takes place in the individual person's mind. Experience is not about individual experiences, disparate pieces of information or systematized data in a human (or technological) hard disk. Experience is constructed socially and collectively on the basis of human action in a particular context.

Thus, to form new experiences about how to handle bullying, the involved individuals have to test new actions and study the effects of these actions. Here common sense would advise actions that – based on experience with "bullying-free" situations – are likely to minimize the participants' experiences of bullying. Parenthetically, there is a considerable body of research that is focused on the opposite: staging events where negative experiences are likely to occur and then studying their effect. That is the case, for example, with the classic experiments that studied how test persons were affected by being ordered to expose other people to electric shock (Milgram, 1974).

Dewey was very aware that the methods we use in our inquiry or in our life practices are not innocuous. Any test of an act and an inquiry into its effects has a moral aspect. Experience formation and inquiry are closely related concepts in Dewey's thinking. Throughout life we form new experiences, and that makes us increasingly able to deal with life's uncertainty and unpredictability.

All scientific knowledge is about relationships between us and the changing environment – not about isolated objects. Thus, the key to everyday experience formation as well as scientific development is the discovery of connections between our actions and their effect in specific situations. New experiences or new scientific findings should not be assessed as to whether they are a precise reflection of reality or on their newsworthiness, but rather on their ability to improve our common conditions. To Dewey, spectator knowledge, which includes the quantified systematization of decontextualized "bullying events", has little chance of predicting what sort of intervention might help improve common conditions in the organization.

Dewey asks how the spectator theory about science has gained such prominence in the Western world. In a possible historical explanation Dewey turns to ancient Greece which had a clear division of labor where women and slaves did the physically demanding manual labor while the free men had both the time and the opportunity to deal with philosophy and theoretical reflection as well as the power to define theoretical reflections as the royal road to true knowledge. This Western distinction between theory and practice and the priority on spectator knowledge over participatory knowledge has its historical background in this social separation between those with theoretical knowledge (intellectual laborers) and those without (physical laborers). Dewey saw this distinction as an obstacle to discovering improvements of the conditions of communities. We will now examine how his thoughts on community are linked with his ideas about morality and ethics.

Developing Morality

To Dewey, all sciences are ethical sciences. As we have discussed before, there is no such thing as a value-free science. Any science must be assessed on its ability to lead to improvements. On ethics, Dewey adopted a middle position in between objectivism and subjectivism. He did not believe that it is possible to set up universal rules for ethical behavior, or that values can be understood separately from human actions and behavior. He also rejected subjectivist theories, which claim that something is good simply because someone likes it or perceives it as good. Brinkmann (2006) calls Dewey's ethical position *pragmatic objectivism*. Brinkmann grounds his use of the term objectivism in Dewey's ideas about the connection between science and ethics. Ethics have scientific aspects: objectivity, a lack of prejudice and an experimental stance. And science, in turn, has ethical aspects, since scientific progress must be assessed on its ability to benefit mankind.

Dewey articulated his ethical vision in the article *Moral Theory and Practice* as early as 1891 (Dewey, 1891). Dewey's rationale for rejecting general ethics theories was that each theory singled out one particular principle as the key to ethical living. Dewey advocated a *pluralistic ethics* based on the idea that any given situation requires the inclusion of many different perspectives to determine which actions may be deemed ethical. This corresponds well with the researchers' thoughts on ethics-in-context which we discussed in Chapter 4.

According to Dewey, general theories of ethics are marred by three flaws: Firstly, they are based on the assumption that ethics can be distinguished from and are something other than human actions. Dewey argued that all actions have an ethical dimension. Since every action is assessed as more or less successful, actions cannot be distinguished from the values that people live by and base their assessments on. This implies an interesting link to Austin's discussion of the conditions that must be in place for speech acts to be considered successful. Thus, in Dewey's thinking ethics is an embedded feature of all human acts.

Secondly, Dewey believed that it was a mistake to perceive ethical theory as something other than an exploration of human actions. In extension of this point, it is also a mistake to see the science of psychology as separate from ethical considerations. We agree. Instead of developing general theories of ethics, the goal should be to achieve moral insight, *"the recognition of the relationships in hand"* (Dewey, 1891, p. 188). Thus, Dewey supports the social constructionist view that ethical considerations must incorporate multiple positions and perspectives and ensure that many voices are included and heard.

Thirdly, Dewey considered it a mistake to view ethical theory as a collection of manuals. Principles cannot be used without reflecting on unique contexts: *"There is no such thing as conduct in general; conduct is what and where and when and how to the last inch"* (Dewey, 1891, p. 191). Actions cannot occur in isolation; they always occur in real-life situations. Here we see how Dewey has paved the way for the concept of context. The application of principles in specific practice contexts requires careful deliberation. Instead of thinking in terms of ideals we should think in terms of conduct and raise questions about what constitutes true, just and loving conduct in the situation at hand. As Dewey so eloquently explains, *"In a word, a man has not to do Justice and Love and Truth; he has to do justly and truly and lovingly. And this means that he has to respond to the actual relations in which he finds himself. To do truly is to regard the whole situation as far as one sees it, and to see it as far as one can; to do justly is to give a fit and impartial regard to each member of this situation, according to its place in the system; to do lovingly is to make the whole situation one's own, not dividing into parts of which one is a warm meum and the other a cold tuum"* (Dewey, 1891, p. 200). The quote illustrates the connection between what is ethical and what is objective. In Dewey's understanding, acting ethically means acting "justly and truly and lovingly" based on a precise analysis of what is objectively required in a specific situation.

Ethical deliberation in a specific situation requires thinking about what might be valuable. Here Dewey distinguishes between what we might desire, and what is desirable. Many individual desires will not necessarily lead to a more desirable life or society. As we shall see, this view is also reflected in Appreciative Inquiry.

Dewey argues that it is neither intelligent nor ethical to follow one's immediate impulses or one's personal preferences or desires. It is not intelligent, as impulses are often arbitrary and inappropriate. And it is not ethical since it is only through deliberation and reflection that we can discover whether an urge or a preference has value or merit. A value judgment does not reflect personal preferences but must be based on an examination that can help us distinguish between desired and desirable. Something is desirable if it enriches our shared life and experiences. Pearce incorporates this notion in his concept of *a better social world* (Pearce, 2007b).

To determine what is desirable we must use thinking and experimental trials, which means testing the conditions and relationships that form the basis for change. The desirable is what changes a situation from problematic to fulfilled or "consummated". Ethical deliberation is crucial in problematic situations. The desirable consists in transforming these into consummated situations – and to do this in a manner that is just, true and loving.

Dewey describes his ethical thinking as *experimental empiricism*. One of the great and recurring concerns in philosophy has been whether it is possible to conclude how things *should be* based on how they *are*. Dewey does not consider this a relevant issue, as it is impossible to divide our experience into, respectively, facts and values. Values are woven into our experience of a given situation; they are not something that is added along the way.

In addition to thinking and experimental trials in specific situations, imagination plays an important role in ethical deliberation. It is our imagination that enables us to entertain possible courses of action. Every situation is unique. It takes judgment and imagination to determine which rule applies in the given situation, and how. That brings us to another important facet of Dewey's view on ethics: Considering whether the use of a rule is meaningful requires a community of practice.

The ability to assess the moral aspects of a situation relies on the habits a person has developed. Dewey says that the sum of these habits constitutes the person's character, and that the most important habit is the ability to assess moral situations. This points to an element of virtue ethics in Dewey's moral philosophy. *"Thus, the fundamental moral question, 'What should I do?' refers back to the even more fundamental question, 'What sort of a person should I be?'"* (Brinkmann, 2004, p. 161; translated for this edition). The point is that a person can only be said to have a good character when the person understands his or her dependence on the community. As members of communities, we are ethically obligated to consider what sort of person we are becoming and what sort of world we are creating.

To guide our ethical deliberation Dewey talks about moments of accomplishment and growth. Moments of accomplishment could also be called moments of consummation, fulfillment or perfection, to use more elevated terms. In Dewey's thinking they are, however, everyday events such as completing a good work effort, ending a chess game or having had a good conversation. With the term growth Dewey refers to events and actions that *expand our meaning-horizon and body of experience*. Here, art may help us see the world better and more clearly. To Dewey, ethics, aesthetics and education are closely related. What, then, constitutes a desirable life? A life that is intelligent, aesthetic and democratic: *Intelligent*, because it is based on the belief that man has the capacity to improve existing conditions by testing knowledge in practice; *aesthetic*, because it is based on a realistic hope that life can be meaningful and contain moments of consummation; and *democratic*, because life is lived in a community with others. A democratic lifestyle helps create a society where *"A democracy is more than a form of government; it is primarily a mode of associated living, of conjoint communicated experience"* (Dewey, 1916/1966, p. 73). Good and growth-promoting communities enable the creation of shared experiences which are facilitated through communication.

Not all communities are necessarily growth-promoting. Dewey carefully distinguishes between undemocratic and democratic communities. The former category includes, for example, Nazi communities and criminal gangs, which may be characterized by an internal set of shared interests, but which isolate themselves and sever all links to the meaning- and value-horizons of other communities. Democratic communities are also moral communities that are capable both of incorporating a wide diversity of shared interests internally and of practicing open and tolerant interactions with other, differently-minded communities.

Dewey has contributed essential concepts and ideas, which have been incorporated into Appreciative Inquiry. This includes, particularly, the emphasis on practical actions in specific situations in communities, the importance of generating participatory knowledge, and the important distinction between individual desires and a desirable future for the whole. These concepts contribute especially to the aspect of *inquiry*. We will now turn to another key source providing useful ideas for the aspect of *appreciation*.

THE ETHICS OF RECOGNITION: AXEL HONNETH

Axel Honneth is a contemporary German philosopher, whose work is gaining increasing international prominence. The key concept in Honneth's authorship is *recognition*. In relation to the sources for *The Struggle for Recognition*,(Honneth, 1995) it is surprising to note that although Honneth's source references include Foucault they do not include authors with roots in social constructionism or Appreciative Inquiry[2].

---

2 A note on terminology: In the English translations of Honneth's work the German word *Anerkennung* is generally translated as *recognition*. When *anerkennung* is translated into Danish is means "anerkendelse" which translates to *appreciation* in English. In discussing Honneth, we use the term *recognition* to avoid confusion in relation to other texts on and by Honneth in English, but we underline here that we see recognition as the basic form of *appreciation*.

Recognition as the Basic Form of Appreciation

How should we understand Honneth's concept of *recognition*? In seeking an answer to this question, a particularly relevant source is the article *Invisibility: On the Epistemology of "Recognition"* (Honneth, 2001). The quotation marks around the term recognition in the title reflect the idea that rendering others invisible is *not* an expression of recognition. Our cultural history is rich in examples of how the powerful in a society could demonstrate their social superiority by failing to "see" people who occupied a lower social position. Servants had to do their job discreetly with no expectation of being "seen". Situations where a person is rendered invisible are, however, not a thing of the past. Cleaning staff will probably recognize this situation: They are doing their job, cleaning an office. An employee, who's looking for his colleague (the person occupying the office) stops by, peeks inside, and says, "Oh, there's nobody here". The employee notes the cleaner's presence but within the context of his meeting with his colleague, the cleaning staff is *nobody*. As this example illustrates, invisibility is not about the lack of sensory perception or about failing to notice that the other person is present. It is not a matter of a lack of perception but of action expressing that A is aware of B's physical presence but does not attribute B any social importance. Correspondingly, B is aware of having been seen and being attributed no social importance. The old saying "Children should be seen and not heard" reflects this form of interaction. When adults said this to children at the dinner table, it meant that they were well aware of the children's physical presence but did not attribute them any social importance, and consequently the children should remain silent. In this example and in many others throughout history the powerful do not always have their way. Those who are rendered invisible have access to a certain repertoire of actions to draw attention to their social existence.

In some cases the people present can agree to ignore or "look right through" each other. In many cultures this may occur in situations when strangers have to share the same space, such as a waiting room or an elevator. Within a Danish setting, strangers usually agree to abstain from direct contact in waiting rooms and elevators. It is important to avoid eye contact in such situations – indeed seeking and maintaining eye contact can be construed as a breach of etiquette. To be able to "look right through" each other requires thorough knowledge of cultural norms and a mastery of appropriate mimicry, gestures and body language. In such situations, invisibility becomes a form of interaction that is culturally agreed upon and the rules of which are carefully negotiated. When the parties are thus in agreement of how to interact, the situation does not lead to humiliation.

Similarly, visibility requires shared knowledge of certain expressive features such as smiles, nods, greetings and gestures. Honneth views visibility as the most elementary form of recognition, the fundamental acknowledgement of someone else's existence. Recognition goes beyond that; it is *"the expressive act through which this cognition is conferred with the positive meaning of an affirmation"* (Honneth, 2001, p. 115).

Expressive body language and gestures carry messages about the parties' relationship and can thus be considered meta-communication or, to borrow Honneth's term: *meta-action*. Rendering the other visible is not just a matter of attributing the person social importance here and now; it also involves an obligation with regard to future interactions, as recognition also signals an intention of friendly actions in the future. By contrast, invisibility lets the other know that he or she cannot expect friendly actions.

In organizations facial expressions and bodily actions constitute an important aspect of social interactions. When two colleagues pass each other in the hallway they greet each other according to the cultural code of conduct that applies in the particular organization. The same is the case by the coffee maker, at lunch, at meetings, and when someone arrives late to a meeting. By nodding, smiling, making verbal greetings, or remaining passive, we express our social relationship with the other and the degree of recognition we award each other.

Through the expressive body actions of recognition we demonstrate a willingness to restrict our egocentric perspective with the purpose of doing justice to the other person's worth. Thus, recognition has a moral core: *"... what is made clear in expressive gestures of recognition is that a subject has already carried out a restriction of her egocentric perspective in order to do justice to the worth of the other person as an intelligible being. To this extent, morality can in a sense even be said to coincide with recognition, because taking up a moral attitude is possible only when the other person is accorded an unconditional worth by which one's own behavior is to be checked"* (Honneth, 2001, p. 123). Note that this form of elementary recognition is not, in Honneth's sense, something that one has to earn. It is a basic human right.

Categories of Moral Disrespect

Honneth's work can be seen as a social critique aiming to highlight how the social forms of communication shape conditions for human identity development. Honneth seeks to explore how a society can achieve solidarity in the sense that it manages to integrate the full range of the citizens' value-horizons, performances and skills. This integration often falls short in our late-modern society where a wide range of experiences of injustice remain invisible in the public debate. In connection with this point, Honneth criticizes his predecessor, Habermas, for not including the many types of moral humiliation that take place: denigration, disrespect, contempt, insult, and unjust treatment. These negative experiences are included in Honneth's analysis as the royal road to defining the nature of recognition. Humiliation and recognition are closely related, as humiliation represents misrecognition or a suspension of recognition.

Honneth classifies moral humiliation in three categories based on the degree of their destructive psychological effect. In this connection Honneth points out that we rely on a number of metaphors for this psychological humiliation, which all spring from bodily decay. The Danish word for humiliation or violation, *krænkelse*, comes from the German word *krank*, which means sick. Disrespect, denigration and humiliation are a threat to a person's identity, just as physical sickness is a threat to our physical survival (Honneth, 1995). Honneth's first category includes acts that rob the person of physical integrity. The most elementary form of personal moral humiliation occurs when someone is forcefully denied the right to freely dispose over their own body. Examples include internment (in the prison system) or being strapped down (in the psychiatric system). Other examples are physical abuse such as violence and rape. Others' disregard for one's physical well-being leads to a loss of trust in oneself and the world. According to Honneth the difference between an act that is perceived as a moral humiliation and an act that is perceived as accidental is precisely the suspension of recognition. An act that causes a person physical pain or discomfort is only perceived as a moral humiliation if it is perceived as deliberate disregard for the person's physical integrity. The same act without this deliberate disregard can be perceived as an accident. Although the physical pain is the same, the major difference lies in the awareness of being or not being recognized. *"Thus, a physical injury becomes a moral injustice if the person affected has no choice but to view it as an action that intentionally disregards an essential aspect of his or her well-being"* (Honneth, 2007, pp. 133-134).

The second category involves types of humiliation that disregard the person's moral responsibility. This occurs when a person is denied certain rights that the person can legitimately expect to enjoy as a member of a community or an institutional order, for example the right to speak or the right not to be exposed to deception or fraud: *"What is specific to such forms of disrespect, as exemplified by the denial of rights or by social ostracism, thus lies not just in the forcible restriction of personal autonomy but also in the combination with the feeling of not enjoying the status of a full-fledged partner to interaction, equally endowed with moral rights"* (Honneth, 1995, p. 133). The disrespect demonstrates that the person is not recognized as a person with moral judgment. This sort of contempt leads to a loss of self-respect or self-esteem.

The third category is the type of humiliation that demonstrates misrecognition of the other's unique abilities. Examples of humiliation in this category range from not greeting another person to outright stigmatization of one or more individuals in the community. A mixed form may be to ignore another person's utterances or to denigrate or ridicule them. This violates the person's sense of having social value to the community in the form of the competences that the person contributes with. This type of humiliation leads to a loss of self-worth.

Recognition/Appreciation as a Moral Obligation

Like John Dewey, Honneth argues for a pluralistic ethics theory. This entails abandoning the idea that the moral quality of actions can be assessed on the basis of an impartial perspective and universal principles. Instead the number of different and at times contradictory expectations, moral obligations and entitlements that we are confronted with on a daily basis makes it necessary for us to integrate a variety of moral perspectives.

Honneth (2007) highlights the close connection between a moral point of view and the mutual obligation of his three forms of recognition. By taking on this obligation we ensure the relational conditions for the formation of identity. This is quite in accordance with Gergen's concept of *mutual relatedness* and the social constructionist idea that the self is shaped in relationships with others (see Chapter 2).

Honneth unfolds how a person's self-image depends on his or her experiences of social recognition. To adopt an ethical position thus entails offering social recognition to others and protecting them from moral humiliation: *"morality is the quintessence of the attitudes we are mutually obligated to adopt in order to secure jointly the conditions of our personal integrity"* (Honneth, 2007, s. 137). This ethical attitude includes mutually independent forms of recognition that can be derived from the previously described forms of moral disrespect.

The first form of recognition is the fundamental *recognition of another person's needs and desires*. In terms of moral philosophy, this recognition constitutes "love" or "care" for someone else's well-being. This emotional and bodily recognition occurs within family relations and friendships and thus belong in the private sphere. This form of recognition is different from the other two by being "conditioned". It requires the presence of close relations that establish emotional bonds among the individuals, and it constitutes the basis for the individual's fundamental self-confidence. The recognition of the other's urges and desires includes the obligations of emotional care that are integrated into all primary relationships such as the asymmetrical relationship between parents and child, and the symmetrical and mutually obligating relationship between friends.

The second form of recognition is *recognizing the other as a person who has the same moral responsibility as everyone else*. This form of recognition is unfolded through our membership of society where we are awarded the same rights as everybody else. Recognition leads to self-respect and an awareness of having the status of an ethically responsible person. These are universal rights and entitlements to equal opportunities. It is this form of recognition that forms the basis for the United Nations' *Universal Declaration on Human Rights*. Unlike the first form of recognition the second does not require the persons to engage in any particular relationship. The recognition of the other's moral responsibility implies the shared obligations to show mutual respect and treat others equally.

The third form of recognition is *recognizing the other's abilities as fundamentally valuable to the community*. This recognition occurs within relationships in groups and political, cultural and work-related communities. The ethical benefits are conditioned by membership of the community. This form of recognition acknowledges the value of the other's unique abilities, skills and contributions and expresses respect for the other's particular importance for the community. It implies mutual moral obligations to cooperation and participation based on a perspective of solidarity.

Honneth emphasizes that a concrete situation may lead to tension between the moral obligations and entitlements, as it may be unclear which form of recognition is at play: *"The moral point of view comprises three moral attitudes that cannot be ranked from one super ordinate vantage point. Thus the entire domain of the moral is pervaded by a tension that can be resolved only in individual responsibility. We are obligated in concrete situations to accord others recognition in a mode that corresponds to the respective kind of social relationship at issue; but in the case of a conflict, we have to decide which of our bonds is to be granted priority according to a different set of guidelines"* (Honneth, 2003, p. 141).

Figure 9: Three Forms of Recognition

	PHYSICAL RECOGNITION	MORAL RECOGNITION	SOCIAL RECOGNITION
PRACTICE AREA	Primary relationships	Citizen in a society	Member of cultural, political and work-related communities
FORM OF RECOGNITION	Recognition of someone's physical existence	Recognition of someone's moral responsibility	Recognition of someone's social value to the community
FORM OF MORAL DISRESPECT	Internment, abuse, violence and rape	Denial of rights and social ostracism	Insult and degradation
MORAL OBLIGATIONS	Emotional support	Mutual respect and the obligation to treat others equally	Mutual obligations to solidarity and cooperation
THE ROLE OF RECOGNITION FOR THE INDIVIDUAL	Self-confidence Physical integrity	Self-respect Social and moral integrity	Self-esteem Personal dignity

To what extent are the three forms of appreciation relevant to life in organizations? As Honneth points out, the first form of recognition belongs in primary relationships. The parents' recognition of the child as worthy of love is crucial for the formation of fundamental self-confidence. This form of recognition is least relevant to life in organizations. There is even a risk that emotional support in the sense of recognizing the other as worthy of love may be perceived as a moral humiliation. Love falls outside the organizational setting, and offering it can seem degrading to the recipient. On the other hand, respect for the individual employee's physical integrity is essential; in an organizational setting that includes providing proper safety conditions and protection from violence and physical abuse.

The second form of recognition: recognizing the individual manager or employee as a morally responsible person is highly relevant to our understanding of the life that unfolds in organizations. When stories about "bullying" or "the destructive boss" are played out in an organization, a common consequence is that a member of the organization is penalized. The appointed bully or the allegedly destructive boss is denied the right to make utterances that are attributed moral validity. In Story 2: *Friendly Concern or Sexual Harassment?* we saw how Hank was denied the opportunity to speak about his experiences and intentions, and how the "victim" and her supervisor no longer considered him morally responsible. This form of moral humiliation is very severe, as it minimizes the person's possibility of contributing to a constructive course of events. When organizational members are denied moral recognition, the possibility of action is often narrowed down to an issue of relocation or dismissal.

The third form of recognition: the recognition of an organizational member's competences and importance for the community is crucial for the ability of all managers and employees to achieve results and make important contributions to the organization. In several of the previous stories it was precisely the denial of a person's ability to make valuable contributions that constituted a moral humiliation. That was the case, for example, in Story 4: *Trial Period Evaluation Turned Therapy* and Story 5: *The Course Participant who was Invited to Reveal Private Information.* Axel Honneth writes that this form of recognition is particularly common in political, cultural and work-related communities. In our mind there is no doubt that the recognition of the individual organizational member's efforts and importance for the work results and the organizational community is crucial both to the individual job satisfaction and to the successful coordination of actions among organizational members. We will now turn to a story with a manager who wanted to make sure that her employees were given the opportunity to perceive themselves as competent and as key contributors to their shared future.

We interviewed the manager, Pamela, a few months after her promotion to mid-level manager of social services in a municipality merged from three smaller municipalities. Pamela, who had been a manager for a few years in the biggest of the three municipalities, was excited about the new job, which would put her in charge of a department of approximately 40 people.

STORY 6: THE MANAGER WHO PUT HER FOOT DOWN WITH THE CONSULTANTS

Once my future appointment was a fact, one of the first things I was told was that an application had been made to the state for funds for consultancy assistance in connection with the merger process, and that the

funding had indeed come through. The application involved several projects. In my department money was allocated for a large-scale competence development project. That sounded fine, but I have to admit it was-
n't one of the first things on my list. I had to get a grasp of my future job
situation, what the conditions were for the department, who the employees were going to be, etc.

At the first meeting with the consultants who were going to be in
charge of the competence development project I was introduced to their
description of the consultancy process. They intended to map the
employee's professional, social and personal competences. They were
planning to have each employee complete a questionnaire and then
carry out one-on-one interviews with a view to uncovering their social
and personal competences. I was somewhat surprised that they were
planning to look at personal competences, and I thought to myself, what
on earth would I want to do with that knowledge? I asked to see the
questionnaire. It had been set up before my time and was based on a list
of the most important tasks in the new department. They had identified
28 individual tasks. For each task the employee was asked to mark their
competence on a five-point scale ranging from "I do this task well" to "I
do this task poorly".

Based on the findings from the questionnaires and the one-on-one
interviews the consultants would then produce a report describing which
competences were present in the department, and which would have to
be developed. I was shocked. How would it affect the employees to have
to complete this questionnaire? Many of the employees I knew had
experience with maybe three or four particular tasks, so they would be in

a situation where they had to mark "poorly" in maybe two dozen tasks – which weren't even relevant to their job description. At first, I was not sure what to do. The consultants had a contract, and I had not been involved in the initial talks. I saw that the findings might produce some insight and perhaps a basis for planning future education efforts. But how would my employees respond? I was not sure what sort of latitude I had. I put the issue aside for a few weeks. I certainly had enough to do. The work load was huge, and we were under a heavy time pressure to get everything sorted out before the deadline of January 1, when the new structure was to be implemented.

Then I took a course in Appreciative Inquiry. The course had been scheduled long before I knew for sure that I would have this new position. It had been a bit of a struggle to keep the dates free in my calendar, but I managed. During the course it became increasingly clear to me that the intended project was completely wrong. The approach the consultants had created to development competencies could never work. First of all, I was increasingly convinced that the resulting "map" of social and personal competences would be on thin ice, for wouldn't those competences depend on the eye of the beholder? Would I afterwards be able to talk with the employees and refer to the particular competences that the consultants had uncovered in their interviews? I didn't think I would want to. And secondly, I became more and more concerned about what effect it would have to complete such a questionnaire about work tasks and professional competences. If someone is given a list of 28 tasks, the person would have to think that I expected him or her to be able to handle all of them – if not now then eventually. And that was far from the case. In the new department there would be many small groups of specialists who certainly would not have to be able to do everything. All the things that the individual employee was unable to do would stand out as he or she was sitting there, marking poorly, poorly, poorly. It was becoming increasingly obvious to me that this might be such a letdown to some of the employees that it would damage their confidence and self-esteem and maybe even make some of them quit. While I was still in the middle of the course, I decided that I would put my foot down.

When I got back to work I scheduled a meeting with the consultants and asked them to carry out the process from an appreciative angle. I did not wish to "map" social and personal competences at all, I did not want a questionnaire about skills in relation to a list of job tasks in the department, and I did not want the focus of the questionnaire to highlight the employees' individual weaknesses. After a lengthy discussion with the consultants the approach was modified; instead they would do group interviews with the employees where they would have an opportunity to talk about what sort of contribution they each might make to the new department. Luckily, the consultants accepted my request.

Before I put my foot down, a downsizing had been decided for my department, and we would have to let four employees go. If the questionnaire survey had been carried out as planned the employees would have to suspect that the four people who were let go were the ones with the most responses of "poorly". And even if I told them that wasn't the case, how could they trust me? I would have a huge credibility issue as a manager. To carry out such a negatively stigmatizing process would go against everything I want to represent as a manager and prevent me

from building good working relationship with my future employees. Today
I am happy that I put my foot down.

Quite in line with Dewey's thinking this manager is convinced that no study
is "for free": There will always be consequences of some kind. Even if she
acknowledges that it might be interesting for her as a manager to learn more
about the competences among the employees in relation to the job tasks of
the new department she is more concerned with the potential effects of
such a study. The consultants in question appear to be working from the traditional deficit perspective, which we will explore in more detail in the last
section of this chapter. From that point of view it is important to identify
the deficits and weaknesses, and use this knowledge as a basis for initiating
improvements – in this case education. The manager instead tries to put herself in the place of employees and wonders how they might feel if they were
put in a situation where they had to reply "I do this poorly" to the majority
of the job tasks on the list. The manager's hypothesis is that it might be a
really bad experience for the employees.

In this story the manager has the courage to "put her foot down". She
demands that the consultants change their approach to an appreciative one
that gives the employees a chance to talk to each other about their contributions to the new work community. This process highlights Honneth's third
form of recognition: recognizing people for their social value to the community.

This manager, like many others, has ethical concerns. She is not only
pondering how to accommodate her employees based on the question,
"What should I do?"; she also considers the fundamental ethical questions,

"What sort of person/manager should I be?" and "What activities are most likely to contribute to a desirable future for the department?" Initially she pushes her notions of discomfort and concern aside and tries to concentrate on the many pressing issues she has to address as a new manager after the merger. With time and with a little outside inspiration from participating in the Appreciative Inquiry workshop she takes her misgivings seriously, takes the time to consider the matter more closely and reaches a radically different decision. Focusing on the employees' strengths and contributions to the department and to the organization becomes the best course of action in this case.

In the next section we will examine how some authors view gut feelings and emotions as a moral compass.

Emotions as a Barometer of Morality

Being exposed to various forms of disrespect can lead to a wide range of reactions, ranging from reactive suffering to proactive action, such as retaliation or more constructive alternatives. What does it take for a moral humiliation to lead to a struggle for recognition? Here, Honneth identifies the negative moral emotional reactions such as disappointment, anger, indignation, shame etc. as important sources of information for someone who has suffered a humiliation. These emotions can facilitate an awareness of having been robbed of social recognition (Honneth, 1995). In support of this point Honneth refers to Dewey's pragmatic psychology, where Dewey emphasizes that emotions should not be seen as an expression of internal states of mind that precede action. Emotions are always associated with actions and with human experiences of successful or failed communication.

Positive emotions occur when someone manages to find a solution that enables subsequent action, while negative emotions such as anger, outrage and grief occur when it is impossible to realize the intended actions. The obstacles may be of a technical or an ethical nature. In the latter case action would lead to the violation of a norm, which makes it difficult to proceed. If it is the subject who has violated the norm the result is a feeling of shame; if it is someone else, the subject may feel a sense of moral indignation. Thus, negative moral emotions may mobilize an active initiative where the wronged person attempts to alleviate the situation. Whether this is the case depends primarily on the political and cultural environment that the wronged person is a part of. According to Honneth the struggle for recognition is a *shared* human struggle.

Honneth's concepts of moral disrespect, experiences of humiliation, and the different forms of recognition are highly relevant in relation to the discussion of moral dilemmas in organizations that is unfolded in the present book. However, Honneth's primary purpose is to contribute to a critical analysis of society – not to study the micro-processes in the unfolding of moral disrespect in human interactions. Nor does he set out to address how people can communicate in ways that help to prevent moral humiliation and promote recognition.

The point about the close link between emotions and morality is also seen in social constructionism, where it is the subject of a substantial body of theory and research. From a social constructionist perspective emotions are seen as embedded in a historical, cultural and context-dependent moral order (Harré & Parrott, 1996; Pearce & Littlejohn, 1997; Gergen, 2005). The close link between emotions and morality has also been addressed in an organizational context, for example in Vincent Waldron's communication studies (Waldron, 2000). In a thought-provoking article titled *Relational Experiences and Emotions at Work* he concludes that emotions in organizations can be considered a barometer for relational ethics. *"Listening carefully to the emotional pulse of an organization should give researchers and members clues to its ethical health. Unemotional organizations, those where emotion is restricted to the private experiences of members, may be those that no longer debate matters of right and wrong"* (Waldron, 2000, p. 79).

How do members of an organization generate good conditions for recognition and appreciation? How do managers and employees enhance their awareness of emotions as a barometer for relational ethics? How do members of an organization enhance their ability to build a better social world? Some answers to these questions can be found in Appreciative Inquiry, which we will turn to now.

Appreciative Inquiry

Appreciative Inquiry is an approach to generating change in organizations and society – an approach that springs from the social constructionist perspective. The first step in what has become a global movement was made in 1987, as David L. Cooperrider and Suresh Srivasta together published the article *Appreciative Inquiry in Organizational Life*. The article was based on the Ph.D. dissertation that Cooperrider had completed in 1986 under Srivasta's supervision. Since then, a large number of theorists and practitioners have contributed to the ongoing development and practical applications of ideas from Appreciative Inquiry. *"Appreciative Inquiry is about the coevolutionary search for the best in people, their organizations, and the relevant world around them. In its broadest focus, it involves systematic discovery of what gives "life" to a living system when it is most alive, most effective, and most constructively capable in economic, ecological, and human terms. AI involves, in a central way, the art and practice of asking questions that strengthen a system's capacity to apprehend, anticipate, and heighten positive potential."* (Cooperrider & Whitney, *A Positive Revolution in Change: Appreciative Inquiry.* 2001)

Today, David L. Cooperrider is a professor of organizational behavior at Case Western Reserve University, and with Kenneth J. Gergen, Mary Gergen, Harlene Anderson, Sheila McNamee, Diana Whitney and Suresh Srivasta he co-founded the Taos Institute, which for years now has served as an important growth center for the ongoing development of Appreciative Inquiry.

Appreciative Inquiry is an approach to management and organizational development. Cooperrider and Whitney (2001) have made the interesting comment on the term that if they were asked to underline one of the two words they would not hesitate to highlight *Inquiry*. In the same article (*A Positive Revolution in Change: Appreciative Inquiry*) they write that the widespread popularity of Appreciative Inquiry is associated with a growing sense that the potential of the traditional problem-solving model is close to exhausted: It is time-consuming, drains energy and usually fails to deliver the desired results. Appreciative Inquiry represents an alternative where the focus is on appreciative and relational processes of experience.

There has been a growing interest throughout the world in applying Appreciative Inquiry in the development of teams, management and organizations with thousands of organizations and groups embracing an appreciative inquiry approach to development and change. And as with all change efforts, some have been successful and others have not. We know of examples of development activities in organizations where some employees felt that Appreciative Inquiry was simply being used to shut them up. Such conduct is very far from the core ideas in Appreciative Inquiry. In the following sections we offer our understanding of these core ideas and a further development of them. Here we shall see that Dewey's thoughts on learning and participatory knowledge and Honneth's ideas about forms of recognition offer important sources of inspiration for this further development.

Appreciative Inquiries into "the Positive"

Appreciative Inquiry has become known for focusing on "the positive". But what does *positive* mean? In a dogmatic black-and-white perspective the answer would be: Look only at exceptional successes and high points. Ignore problems. Talk only about your successes and what is valuable. Do not be blinded by the obstacles in a given situation. Look only at the possibilities.

We take a different view. Upon closer inspection we find that the word *positive* has several meanings. Firstly, it can refer to what is, exists or takes place. This fundamental meaning of the word is important in our interpretation of Appreciative Inquiry. An example: A young woman goes to her doctor for a pregnancy test and calls to check the result. She is told that the test is positive, which means that the analysis suggests that she is pregnant. The test found that there "is" something. Thus, it is a finding that something exists.

Secondly, the word *positive* can mean the existence of something that we find valuable or desirable. To one woman, a positive pregnancy test can be a very positive and exciting result; to another it may represent a very negative and disconcerting result. Thus, positive can also refer to the aspects that are considered valuable and desirable from a particular perspective.

Thirdly, the word refers to something that we are capable of creating and engaged in realizing, that is, the potential or that which is becoming.

All three meanings of the word *positive* are relevant to Appreciative Inquiry. The first is the most important in relation to the original ideas in Appreciative Inquiry. The focus is on past and current actions and events that emphasize when we are doing our best, and on what can we glean, learn from and derive from these experiences. This is where the inspiration from John Dewey is most apparent: Learning springs from experience in concrete situations. Thus, in an Appreciative Inquiry we are learning from what is happening when we are doing our best and trying to distill from those moments of everyday complexity what is desirable and possible.

In this mode of inquiry, we are switching our focus from what is absent, undesirable and impossible to what exists, what is desirable and what is possible. This can be a challenging task for most of us. For example, in courses in communication where the participants are asked to study examples of appreciative communication, we often notice the inclination to offer feedback about what is *not*. For example, utterances such as "How come you didn't ask ..." or "It would have been interesting to hear more about ..." We are well versed in identifying the shortcomings in our own and others' efforts, but it takes a particular mental effort to notice what is happening that is good and works well, which effects it has on creating a positive outcome, and where it might lead.

Appreciative Inquiry offers an alternative to the traditional problem-solving, which is often used in organizational change. One of the differences between the two approaches is their assessment of what is important to study and learn more about. *"Human systems grow in the direction of what they persistently ask questions about."* (Cooperrider & Whitney, 2001). Thus if we ask questions about the problems within a systerm we will grow in the direction of those problems and if we ask questions about strengths, assests, innovations, high points, and possiblities, we will grow in the direction of these ideas and practices. These differences in emphasis can be summarized as follows:

Figure 10: What do we want to study and learn about?

TRADITIONAL PROBLEM-SOLVING	APPRECIATIVE INQUIRY
Absent actions and events Shortcomings	The best of the past and existing actions and events
The undesirable Errors and what should be avoided	The desirable What should be achieved
The impossible (barriers, obstacles)	The possible

Appreciative Inquiry considers it quicker, more direct and more respectful to focus on the best of the past, the existing, the desirable and the possible. Traditional problem-solving and Appreciative Inquiry are quite different approaches to creating change especially when it comes to what we focus on – as illustrated by a statement David L. Cooperrider made at a seminar: *"Behind every problem there's a dream waiting to be brought to life."* Detailed investigations into the many causes of errors and problems rarely offer insight into visions of a desirable future. The main challenge is to find an affirmative frame that preserves the link between problem and dream – a frame that can open the door to an inquiry into what is most desirable. Let us look at an example where an employee consulted her coach because she felt stressed and close to her breaking point:

STORY 7: THE EMPLOYEE WHO CONSULTED HER COACH ABOUT STRESS

I went to see my coach because I needed help managing my job situation, which was getting out of hand. A couple of my coworkers had broken down due to stress, and I was worried that I might be headed that way myself. I had far too many things on my plate, I was basically never off work, and I was thinking about work the whole time. In my company we have flexible work hours, and your job is what you make it, so I had worked hard to amass a lot of assignments in order to be a visible competence in the workplace. Now it was too much, and I knew that I had to start turning assignments down. At the same time I really didn't want to turn anything down, as I worried that my colleagues and clients might stop bringing me work.

So my request to my coach was help to learn to turn requests down to keep from going under.

In the coaching session the coach first asked me to talk a little bit about the background for my request. I told her that I had difficulty managing my work situation, often felt overwhelmed, overburdened, stressed, and had difficulty turning assignments down. Then she asked me which of my current assignments I was most excited about, and why. That was a challenging question; I hadn't really given that much thought

– I just took everything that landed up on my desk.

I realized that there were certain things about an assignment that made it appealing to me. Some of these features included: if the assignment lay within my particular field of interest, where I would like to be known as a capacity; if there was enough time for the assignment, so that I could do a better than mediocre job; if I could work with those of my colleagues that I knew I could learn from; and if hardly anybody else would be able to do the assignment. Gradually, I realized what was important in my work, and what it was that I really liked.

Then my coach asked me what would happen if I actively accepted the assignments that lived up to my requirements. I saw immediately that this would mean fewer assignments and far greater job satisfaction for me. That in turn would lead to a higher quality in my work, which would also be in the company's interest. It was a huge relief to see this possibility. But I was still worried about what would happen to the assignments I didn't accept. The coach asked me to explore those times when and how I had previously managed to turn down an assignment, in part or in full, in a good way. I was only able to come up with a couple of examples. So we talked about them and discovered that I could actually offer additional reasons for why the assignment should not be mine and that in many cases I might still be able to help the person who asked for my assistance by suggesting who might take the assignment instead. That was important to me, since I had previously associated turning down an assignment with the total rejection of a client or a colleague, which of course I didn't want. But now I saw that there were many alternatives to simply rejecting or accepting the assignment.

Initially, I had thought that I needed to learn to say "no" to keep from being too stressed, but now I was thinking that I would only say "yes" to the right assignments and help get the remainder placed with the right competence in the workplace.

That was a bit of an eye-opener. I have used the method on later occasions, and it has become much clearer to everybody, including myself, what my core competences are – in fact, I'm now known as a specialist in exactly the areas that I am most interested in working on. I still have a lot of work, but while my assignments used to be a very mixed bag, and many of them were boring and less important to the company, now they are more prestigious assignments that are also right up my alley. So at the same time as I am in higher demand, I'm having much more fun, and I'm not under as much pressure as I was before. I no longer worry about stress. I'm just busy with assignments that are important, make a real difference, help develop my competences, and are fun.

This employee is experiencing great changes that are of personal importance to her. How is this accomplished? In a traditional problem-solving approach a coach would ask about the nature of the stress (how many specific symptoms?), its extent (how big a part of your work day and for how long?), the negative consequences (how severe is it?) and its causes (why are you under so much stress?). In addition, a problem-solving coach might focus on why the employee fails to turn down assignments. Does she lack the courage, the self confidence or the communication skills? The coach in this story does none of these things. We see an appreciative approach to coaching. One of the first questions from the coach invites the employee to talk about the assignments that are most exciting to her, which then led to an exploration of the criteria for energy-building assignments. One of the next questions was a hypothetical question, directed at what might happen if the employee accepted the assignments that met her criteria. As we see, these few questions invite the employee to explore a desirable future rather than studying problems and causes in the past. Then follows an exploration of the potential consequences of turning down the low-priority assignments. This in turn leads to a shift away from thinking about a personal problem (stress) to thinking about possible actions and responsibility for many actors in a larger work community. During this process the employee is able to see her own experiences and competences more clearly, while an emphasis on the causes of stress and her reasons for not saying "no" would probably have put issues of personal inadequacies on the agenda. We see how Honneth's third form of recognition (social recognition) is put into play during the session.

A traditional problem-solving approach is often characterized by positioning the involved persons as victims. That could have been the case in this coaching session as a result of questions about the severity of the stress. But that is not what happened. Instead, the appreciative approach helped the employee discover several options and her ability to speak as a moral agent who was responsible for her choices and obligated to consider the consequences for others – colleagues and clients. Thus, Honneth's second form of recognition (moral recognition) is also at play here with the result that the employee leaves the session strengthened and with a clear picture of what needs to happen.

The story also illustrates the important point that appreciation is strongly conducive to new insights.

Thus, Appreciative Inquiry is not about producing new knowledge about what does not work but about generating respectful processes of experience in relation to the existing, desirable and possible. When we choose to inquire into moments and experiences of success, when we are most alive and contributing to the organization, we learn, grow and move towards our best images of a positive future. To clarify what is unique about Appreciative Inquiry we offer the model below:

Figure 11:
Four Approaches to Organizational Development

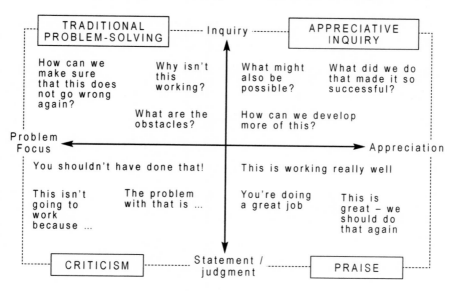

(Freely based on Hammond, 1996)

In the figure the vertical axis illustrates the dimension of inquiry versus statement/judgment, while the horizontal axis illustrates problem focus versus appreciation. Let us first turn to the two lower quadrants where communication takes the form of statements or judgments of actions and events that are either seen as negative or positive, that is, judgments that offer criticism or praise. We use both *statement* and *judgment* as the two forms which are often difficult to tell apart in everyday communication. What one person perceives as a matter-of-fact statement, such as "The problem is that you didn't spend enough time on the project," is easily seen as a judgment by the person at the receiving end.

In a common-sense understanding praise is closely related to appreciation. It is nice for a manager or an employee to be told that others appreciate something they said or did. Appreciation can help heighten the awareness of the desirable in an organization and enhance working relationships among organizational members. However, when appreciation comes in the form of a statement with no inquiry element, the learning potential is limited. To be told, "You did great," is very reassuring and makes us want to do more of the same, but in itself it offers no information about exactly what made the performance so good. When appreciation is combined with inquiry the concept of appreciation takes on new meaning: Appreciation is based on the belief that every manager, employee or consultant contributes with resources and competences and basically has good intentions and a sincere desire to contribute. Praise, on the other hand, is about assessing others based on one's *own* standards or assumptions. It risks creating a subject-object relationship where the person awarding the praise positions him/herself as a subject and the person receiving the praise as an object.

Judgments can also be negative, as illustrated in the lower left quadrant. "You shouldn't have done that" contains a negative judgment or perhaps even a condemnation. Criticism has an even smaller learning potential than praise. Praise can encourage a person to repeat the action that was assessed positively. Criticism, by contrast, does not encourage anything. If the criticism comes in the form of "You shouldn't have done that," the recipient has nothing to work with, since it contains no information about which actions to choose instead of the one that was criticized. That risks draining energy and reducing the motivation to ask follow-up questions. As in the case of praise, criticism is at considerable risk of generating a subject-object relationship.

In relation to organizational development it is crucial to consider the learning potential of the four different approaches. The two lower quadrants mainly involve statements and responses. In the education system and in many organizational cultures our ability to come up with answers is more appreciated than the ability to listen and ask good questions. At first glance, a person may seem more competent when offering an unequivocal answer than when asking a difficult question. Delivering answers is often accompanied by a feeling of being knowledgeable and in control, while asking questions is often seen as a sign of confusion, ignorance or a lack of understanding. To practice working from an Appreciative Inquiry perspective, however, one has to resist the temptation to appear smart, maybe smarter than others, by providing answers. In this approach, being smart is more about asking appreciative and explorative questions and about listening carefully for the potential embedded in the replies. It is about being open to the conversation and about seeking out what is happening when we are doing our best.

In the top two quadrants – traditional problem-solving and Appreciative Inquiry – the emphasis is on asking questions. In the next section we take a closer look at what characterizes good questions and at the rationale behind the two approaches, particularly with regard to exploring the learning potential.

Appreciative Inquiry as an Alternative to Traditional Problem-Solving

In Western culture, it is a common understanding that scientific progress consists of identifying things that can potentially be wrong with people, organizations and societies. Scientific development is so strongly based on a language focused on problems and deficiencies that a research finding that leads to the launch of a new diagnosis can be as important as the discovery of a new star in the universe (Cooperrider & Whitney, 2001). The British author Aldous Huxley (1894-1963) is often quoted for saying, *"Medical science has made such tremendous progress that there is hardly a healthy human left."* Progress in medical science is not just about improving treatment options but also about improving the ability to describe in detail anything a person can possibly suffer from. Psychology and psychiatry have similarly improved their ability to place people in a growing number of categories depending on what ails them. The conviction that we acquire wisdom by having access to an arsenal of error categories and precise methods for classifying people according to these categories is deeply rooted in Western culture.

The traditional problem-solving model in organizations leans heavily on the concept of errors and shortcomings and is based on a common-sense understanding that problems are solved when errors and deficiencies and their causes are identified (Haslebo & Nielsen, 2000). Appreciative Inquiry represents an alternative in its focus on *what is* and *what could be*. This does not imply turning a blind eye to the many problems that managers and employees experience in their organization: *"Appreciative Inquiry is a complex science designed to make things better. We can't ignore problems – we just need to approach them from the other side"* (Cooperrider & Whitney, 2001, p. 11). What, then, is "the other side"? Briefly put, the answer is to study and learn about what we is happening when we are doing our best and to explore what we want to bring about rather than what we want to *avoid*. We will return to this point of view later after first offering a concrete example of the workings of the traditional problem-solving approach in practice and the fundamental assumptions it rests on.

The example is inspired by the Danish psychologists Mette Borg Jensen and Kirsten Jespersen's master's dissertation on a system for reporting unintended events as a learning measure in the Danish hospital sector (Jensen & Jespersen, 2005). Here, the authors address a serious problem: Every year, approximately 9% of all hospital patients in Denmark are exposed to unintended events, that is, ill effects that are not due to their condition but to inadequate or erroneous treatment by the medical employees (Schiøler et al., 2001). Some of the errors are relatively insignificant, while others can prolong hospitalization (for example in the case of erroneous medication) or, in the worst case, lead to permanent impairment or even death. The issue of increasing patient safety is high on the political agenda.

Denmark was one of the first countries in the world to pass legislation on patient safety in the health care system. The law came into effect in 2004. The stated objective is to *"create learning to reduce the amount of unintended events"* (www.patientsikkerhed.dk/loven; translated for this edition). Along with the law, a reporting system for unintended events was launched that had been developed by the Danish National Board of Health. In this system, errors are called *unintended events*, which are defined as follows: *"An unintended event is an event resulting from treatment or stay in a hospital and not from the illness of the patient, if such event is harmful or could have been harmful if it had not been prevented (…) Unintended events shall comprise events and errors known and unknown"* (Act on Patient Safety in the Danish Health Care Sector, 2003, section 2). Prior to the development of the reporting system a major effort was undertaken to identify methods that would help reduce the number of unintended events. This effort included focus group interviews and questionnaire surveys with 2,000 participating nurses and doctors, who were asked to share their wishes and recommendations. Based on this and other sources, it was decided that it should be possible to report unintended events in confidentiality and without the risk of sanctions for the person making the report or anyone else. The reported information would be stored in a central database and categorized with regard to type, frequency, etc. The most serious or frequent unintended events would be subjected to a root-cause analysis. Next, the results of the categorizations and the root-cause analyses would be reported to the level of the individual hospital to enable those responsible for patient safety to undertake appropriate preventive measures. These measures would consist of newsletters, quarterly reports, campaigns and guidelines.

The act made it mandatory for hospital staff to report unintended events. The interesting point now was: Would they? A year and a half later, it was found that they would – and in far greater numbers than expected. The system was a success in the sense that 5,740 reports were made to the National Board of Health in 2004. In March 2005, when the first annual report was issued, a briefing from the director-general stated, *"The annual report also shows that, despite guidelines from the National Board of Health, unintended events continue to occur in some areas. The report from the Danish Society for Patient Safety also point out certain types of events that are typical, and which have been targeted in various ways without a satisfactory result"* (newsletter from Sundhedsstyrelsen (Danish National Board of Health, 2005); translated for this edition). The guidelines were rarely followed. The employees appeared to achieve little learning that led to any improvement in patient safety; and this despite the fact that the system and the procedures were based on a clear model of the learning process consisting of 1) observation, 2) documentation, 3) analysis, 4) prediction and 5) prevention.

Why is the outcome in terms of learning about the prevention of unintended events so meager when the reporting system is seeing far more use than expected? That was the issue that the psychologists Jensen and Jespersen (2005) set out to explore based on various theories on learning. Based on a theoretical analysis the authors reach the interesting conclusion that the reporting system rests on fundamental assumptions that, contrary to the intentions, reduce the likelihood that the employees will actually learn and change their behavior. We will explore this analysis further and highlight some of the key assumptions:

Key assumptions
in a system for reporting errors

- To err is human.
- Errors are individual acts that deviate from a standard.
- Errors are unavoidable.
- Individuals will defend themselves against criticism for committing an error.
- Guilt and shame do not promote learning. Therefore the causes of errors should be found in the circumstances.
- Information on errors (unintended events) can be taken out of the concrete situation and processed statistically while still remaining meaningful.
- Knowledge consists in being able to describe general connections between errors and causes.
- Individuals can acquire new knowledge about the general connections between errors and causes through reading.
- When individuals acquire new knowledge they will change behavior.

These assumptions are all challenged from a social constructionist perspective.

Indisputably, the reporting system is based on considerable efforts to create a system that would not lead to an inappropriate attribution of guilt and shame. As we saw, the effort to make hospital staff report unintended events was successful. Nevertheless, we see that these assumptions are mainly based in realism, an individualist perspective and the view of communication as a transmission of knowledge from mind to mind.

As we saw in Chapter 2, according to a realist perspective it is possible to draw a precise and adequate image of a subject area. Not only is it possible; it is essential. Once we know the incidence of various events, the characteristics of each type of event, its frequency and its causes, we will be able to alter the outcome. This is exactly the same logic we saw applied in the research about bullying (see Chapter 5). The individual perspective is also apparent. It is the individual who delivers data, and the individual who reads the guidelines and consequently acquires learning that leads to changes in behavior. The emphasis on guidelines is based on the view of knowledge as something that can be possessed and transferred from one person to another.

Jensen and Jespersen's work is valuable because it can be used to reassess the rationale on which the reporting system is based. Without this reassessment it is highly likely that noting the failure to achieve the desired result (fewer unintended events) will simply lead to more of the same. Conclusions based on the fundamental assumptions mentioned above might be as follows: "The number of categories of unintended events must be increased, the root-cause analyses must be refined, and the guidelines need to be expanded and offer more details". However, we doubt that more of the same will to lead to different and better outcomes. To achieve a better result becomes possible when working on a different set of fundamental assumptions. Let us consider the underlying assumptions about learning and development in from an Appreciative Inquiry perspective.

Underlying Assumptions in Appreciative Inquiry

- Learning in an organization is related to concrete experiences in a community of practice when we coordinate our own actions with those of other organizational members.
- The actions and events in the organization that we study are the ones we learn about and the ones that we will focus on for further growth.

- What we focus on becomes a bigger part of our shared reality.
- In any organization there is something that works well.
- There is more energy and direction in learning about and focusing on the things we do well and the things we want more of than focusing on the things we do not do well and do not want.
- Problematic situations arise in an organization when it is difficult for the organizational members to coordinate their actions.
- Appreciative Inquiry is about asking questions based on the conviction that others have good reasons for doing what they do.
- Asking appreciative questions will bring out the best in others and enhance relationships within the organization as a whole.
- Appreciative communication is based on the assumption that other organizational members have something important and valuable to contribute.
- Learning that leads to a better coordination of action requires mutual dialogue among the participants in the specific community of practice.

A development of methods aimed at promoting patient safety based on these assumptions would lead to a completely different set of considerations. Here we will offer a few ideas.

Firstly, we might turn to Cooperrider's idea of finding an affirmative frame for what we want to study. Cooperrider calls this Topic Choice. We can choose to inquire into experiences within the system when an error was prevented. Focusing on successful patient safety rather than experiences where errors were prevalent will help us improve patient safety. We can ask questions such as: What was happening in this situation that created total patient safety? At the time the error was about to occur, what risks were averted and how? Who was involved in bringing about the safest outcome for this situation? Which actions worked well? What did the involved persons learn?

Secondly, if we a shift our thinking from an individual perspective to a perspective that sees unintended events as an outcome of difficulties with coordination, how would this lead to considerations about how new methods might facilitate mutual communication and joint learning processes within the department. Individuals do not work alone, we are continually coordinating our efforts and actions. Here Dewey's concept of *participatory knowledge* is helpful. The key is to promote opportunities for the involved parties' to learn together within the specific situations rather than producing spectator knowledge where disparate information is processed in a centralized data processing system based on the assumption of a universal link between cause and effect. In extension of this, we need to focus instead on creating the necessary time and conditions for dialogue within and between the departments, across professional groups, and on developing the necessary competences for an inquiry into what is happening when we are doing our best.

Thirdly, it would be important to consider how new methods for coordinating actions might promote a moral responsibility for doing something in the many risky and variable everyday events as they unfold rather than living up to a formal obligation to report unintended events after they have occurred.

We will now explore how the reporting system in question also affects the definition of moral obligations and entitlements.

Responsibility and Moral Obligations

The conflicting results of the use of the reporting system for unintended events in hospitals also seem puzzling in light of the fact that patient safety is a target that everybody – employees, patients, families and citizens – finds extremely important. Jensen and Jespersen (2006) mention a study which showed that one third of all doctors and nurses at times considered leaving their profession as they were afraid of being involved in unintended events. However, many of the people who use the system like it and feel relieved to have an outlet that they can use when they experience frustration and unsatisfactory events in their everyday work. As an example, the authors mention a situation where a nurse notices that a doctor fails to wash his hands before he examines the next patient. In that situation it may seem like a relief to be able to act by reporting the incident. However, the relief of being able to report such an incident can have serious negative consequences. If we consider the reporting system as a narrative and consider how it positions the organizational members, we can derive a set of hypotheses about how reality is constructed. The emphasis that the system places on circumstances sends a message to the employees that they are innocent victims of circumstance: With circumstances being what they are, the individual employee cannot escape the occurrence of unintended events. As mentioned earlier, the purpose of focusing on circumstances rather than individuals is to avoid making the erring person feel guilt and shame and hence be reluctant to provide information about the unintended event. The error-producing circumstances are considered to be created by the system, that is, the result of strategic management decisions in terms of time pressures, understaffing, inferior equipment, etc. In our view, this mindset simply means that guilt and shame are assigned to the management level, while the employees go free.

If we treat this reporting system as a narrative, we find four positions:

1. The attentive and blame-free hospital employee who reports on him/herself or others as the cause of an error.
2. The employee who is reported for being involved in an unintended event – possibly without knowing about this.
3. The key individuals responsible for patient safety and for providing information and guidance.

Management whose job it is to alter the error-producing circumstances.

The system defines the parties' moral obligations and entitlements in a very interesting manner. The employee who makes the report is alleviated of the obligation to act in the specific situation. It is enough to report that the doctor did not wash his hands. The system does not obligate the nurse to do anything in the situation, for example by alleviating the time pressure the doctor might be under or reminding him to wash his hands. The relief that Jensen and Jespersen describe is understandable from the perspective of this positioning. The employees are relieved of their bad conscience by being able to act as responsible observers and informants in relation to unintended events. The employee has a moral obligation to notice harmful or potentially harmful incidents but is not required to notice the events that lead to a good result. The attention is aimed at what should be avoided, not at what should be achieved. In subtle ways, this attentive focus and the obligation to record and note risks relieve the employees of any moral responsibility to act in relation to other organizational members in the specific situation.

That eliminates an opportunity to learn about how we can communicate with others in everyday situations to avoid unintended events. In summary: The reporting system is a success, but the effects in terms of learning and of reduction of errors is minimal.

If patient safety is to be improved, an important aspect in the development of new methods will be to consider how these can involve an appreciation of the hospital staff as morally responsible agents whose obligations involve assuming responsibility in the given situation and acting as co-creators of the situation – rather than living up to a formal obligation.

INQUIRY OF VALUE TO THE WORK COMMUNITY

We will now attempt to summarize the points of this chapter in a moral obligation that we call *inquiry of value to the work community*. This implies a particular quality of ethical considerations. It is not enough to ponder and analyze a situation from a linear perspective. Inquiry in a social constructionist understanding springs from a circular perspective that considers the moral dilemmas from multiple positions and perspectives, and which includes one's own position and contributions to the co-creation of the social reality. *Inquiry of value to the work community* underlines the importance of assessing one's own and others' actions based not on value to oneself, but to the entire work community – that is, the extent to which the actions help create a desirable future. We will now unfold some of the key ideas of this moral obligation.

In the introduction to this chapter we explained Dewey's thoughts on the ever-changing nature of the world. Basic assumptions about change have significant consequences for how moral obligations are defined. Dewey's thinking represents an alternative to the traditional view on change that prevails to this day; a view that describes change as the transition from one stable situation to a new stable situation. The understanding of the stable situation is objectified in the sense that it is considered important to be able to offer a precise description of the qualities that characterize both the original situation and the end goal. Change is seen as a difficult transition to a new normal state; this view invites an instrumental approach that aims to find efficient methods for getting the process over with as quickly as possible in order to arrive at the desired state. The dominant discourse on change management that we discussed in Chapter 5 is based on these assumptions, which lead to the widespread technical-rational strategy of change. This strategy implies that it is essential to put experts who are familiar with efficient technologies in charge of bringing the organization through the phase of transition. The experts (consultants and managers) are positioned as subjects, while the employees and remaining managers are positioned as objects to be guided through the transition without too much resistance. The objectified employees are entitled to criticize the duration and nature of the transition phase and the obligation to take a positive attitude toward the intended future situation.

Dewey had a very different view on change. He emphasized the ever-changing nature of the world and saw everyday events as inevitably variable, fleeting, impermanent and unpredictable. In this lens, it is more meaningful to see events as processes that people are involved in and co-create. Thus, we should pay attention to everyday episodes and actions. Here we remind the reader of the quote by Pearce in Chapter 3, with his ironic comment on our low community standards for "quality control" of the individual episodes in everyday life.

Firstly, inquiry of value to the work community is thus about enhancing our awareness of the *ethical aspects of the ongoing flow of events in everyday life* and seeking to discover connections between what we do in interactions with others and the effects our actions have on others. This is a crucial point in social constructionism and in Appreciative Inquiry, where it is considered an important challenge to use language and communication in ways that bring out and highlight collaborative experiences, competences and practical wisdom. The notion that we co-create each other through language contains a moral obligation to consider how our communicative actions can help bring out the best in each other. This point relates to Honneth's third form of recognition (social recognition) which focuses on how members of a community of practice can contribute to the community.

Secondly, inquiry of value to the work community focuses on the question, "How can I/we contribute to improving conditions for the work community?" Dewey draws a clear distinction between individual desires and a desirable future. Discovering how a desirable future might look is no simple matter; it requires a careful exploration of the specific situation with the relationships that it involves. That poses a major moral challenge that also plays a key role in Appreciative Inquiry, which has contributed a rich development of methods for promoting dialogues among organizational members with a view to discovering how they can move toward a desirable future.

Thirdly, inquiry of value to the work community is about growth in Dewey's understanding of the word. As described previously, Dewey defines growth as an *expansion of the agents' meaning-horizon and body of experience.* Thus, growth is a qualitative term that is very different from our current focus on quantitative measures of change and development. We addressed this issue in the discourse on documentation and evaluation in Chapter 5. Let us offer an example of the high priority on quantitative growth that is applied not only in relation to growth in turnover and market shares but also in relation to personal development. In a private company a new concept for management evaluation was introduced that contained a wide range of activities such as business-oriented tests, team building and training courses. The success in terms of management development would be documented by an annual rise of 0.5% in employee evaluations of the individual manager on a number of facets to be rated on a five-point scale. In our opinion that is simply numerical mumbo jumbo. What sort of meaning and importance can possibly be represented by a statistical average of 0.5%? How is it possible to take this 0.5% rise to mean that managers and employees have learned anything? Indeed, that may not be the intention. Perhaps, the success criterion of 0.5% is an instrument of control to ensure that the managers agree to take part in the scheduled activities out of fear of their next staff evaluation – and perhaps also to justify the existence of the HR department.

Fourthly, inquiry of value to the work community implies a moral obligation to recognize others as morally responsible co-agents. Honneth's ideas about the second form of recognition are of essential importance here. In studying the extensive literature on Appreciative Inquiry, we find that its main emphasis is on appreciating others as competent contributors to the achievement of job goals and to the cooperation within organizations, while the recognition of others as moral agents has a less prominent status. However, we are convinced that this latter form of recognition is taking on increasing importance in organizations. To adopt the position that other organizational members may have important ethical reasons for their actions is also a moral obligation. In extension of this point, increasing our curiosity toward these ethical reasons becomes more important than judging and holding organizational members accountable for their actions or sins of omission. Again, the mutual recognition of each other as moral agents requires a respectful dialogue.

REFLECTIONS

In this chapter we have looked at John Dewey's ideas about inquiry and Axel Honneth's ideas about various forms of recognition. We have turned to these two thinkers both in order to find new ways of understanding the mutual relatedness in organizations and to contribute to the ongoing development of Appreciative Inquiry. We consider Appreciative Inquiry a very powerful approach to constructing mutually respectful relationships and shared learning and finding practical ways of taking on the obligation to engage in dialogue.

We have identified a number of moral obligations, which we have summarized under the term inquiry of value to the work community. We have thus progressed a bit in the exploration of how organizational members can contribute to creating better social worlds.

As we have previously discussed, the possibility to co-create each other and to appear as moral agents is rarely evenly distributed in organizations. At this point we must address the concept of power and study the impact of different understandings of the concept on the issues addressed in this book. This is thus the topic of our next chapter.

CHAPTER 7

POWER AND MORAL RESPONSIBILITY

Power is a key concept in social constructionism, and it plays an important role in relational ethics. In previous chapters we have discussed how organizational members have unequal opportunities for influencing the unfolding of everyday events. In Chapter 2 we discussed the basic assumption in social constructionism that power consists in the ability to define reality and what constitutes knowledge. In a common-sense understanding based on realism, power is seen as a property residing in the individual – a property that is expressed as the control over other people's actions. By contrast, a social constructionist perspective views power as a relational phenomenon that is co-created in everyday patterns of communication. In Chapter 3 we mentioned that members of an organization do not have the same opportunities for carrying out socially responsible actions. That was illustrated, for example, in Story 2: *Friendly Concern or Sexual Harassment?* where Hank, who was accused of being a villain, had more difficulty making his voice heard than Diane, who was the accusing victim. As Hank was excluded from having his voice heard, he was less able to shape constructive speech acts and build contexts where the parties might be able to coordinate their actions and move on in a shared everyday life. In Chapter 5 we continued along the same path by illustrating how a variety of discourses and narratives shape relationships that are either mutually respectful or not. In the latter, the relationship is defined by involving a subject who has the right to produce knowledge about the object and defining what constitutes valid knowledge about it. We also demonstrated how discourses and concrete stories imply an embedded power to position oneself and others in more or less beneficial ways.

In this chapter we will continue to explore and unfold these aspects of the concept of power. First, we offer a brief introduction to Michel Foucault's thoughts on modern power, the disciplining of the individual as an object, and the shaping of the individual as subject. Next, we describe how Michael White has developed Foucault's thoughts and used them in his clinical practice. Neither Foucault nor White looked at the exercise of power on microlevels in organizations. Nevertheless, we intend to demonstrate the relevance of many of the ideas in an organizational setting. We will discuss the following questions: How can we understand events in organizations if we view them in a perspective of power? How are power and morality connected? How are unequal opportunities shaped by discourses and narratives? How are various practices used in organizational and management development related to power? How are they involved in defining a manager's moral obligations and entitlements? And how are employees' moral obligations and entitlements defined? First, we will look at Foucault's thoughts on power.

TRADITIONAL VERSUS MODERN POWER

Foucault's thinking on power has been tremendously influential in the development of both the social and human sciences. Michel Foucault was French and lived from 1926 to 1984. Foucault studied philosophy and psychology and was a philosopher by profession. He did not like to pick any single label for his work. Although he was the author of many books, he did not like to refer to himself as an author and certainly not a guru. He saw his work as a tool box, for which he did not like to dictate the use; he considered himself a navigator or a toolmaker (Heede, 2004). Foucault set out to demonstrate how people have historically and culturally been shaped by their contexts.

Throughout his work, Foucault was not interested in a theory of power, the essence of power or the intentions of those performing power, but rather in the exercise of power on an everyday level and in the effects on people of the exercise of power.

Foucault distinguished between traditional and modern power. It is a key point in his thinking that modern power has historically held a much stronger position than traditional power. Below, we offer a summary of the differences between these two types of power. The presentation is inspired by White (2002).

Figure 12: Characteristics of Traditional versus Modern Power

TRADITIONAL POWER	MODERN POWER
Social control is exercised through institutionalized moral judgments by appointed representatives of the state and its institutions	Social control is exercised through normalizing judgment by people in the evaluation of their own and each other's lives
Power socializes people to strive for moral worth	Power socializes people to strive for normative worth
Power is located at a center and is exercised from the top down	Power is located in disparate and shifting coalitions and alliances on a local level
Power is repressive	Power is productive
People perceive themselves as being outside power and subjected to it	Power recruits people into activities that involve surveillance and control of their own and each other's lives
The spotlight is aimed at the center of power and renders visible coercion and punishment as forms of power	The spotlight is aimed at the lives of individuals, thus rendering invisible the disparate and shifting function of the exercise of power
The spotlight is aimed at the center of power, thus rendering invisible the individuals who are subjected to coercion or punishment	The spotlight is aimed at the lives of individuals, thus letting them know that their lives may at any time be made the object of scrutiny and public judgment
A technology is employed that is characterized by symbols of influence (ceremonies, pomp, public punishment, etc.)	A technology is employed that establishes a continuum of normality/abnormality, performance tables, scales for rating human behavior, etc.

Traditional power systems operate out of a center, from the top down, by means of institutionalized systems of coercion. Power is about the right to carry out moral judgments of other people's actions as being right or wrong, good or bad, moral or immoral. Traditional power is institutionalized and aims to restrict, inhibit, prohibit or rule out actions that are deemed immoral. In this view, power is repressive. The understanding of power as negative and repressive remains widespread in organizations to this day. These forms of power are exercised by a "system", which individuals are outside and may protest against. The reflections on visibility are interesting. Traditional exercise of power is visible and relies on ceremony, public performances with pomp and circumstance, and public punishment. No one should be left in any doubt about the reality of the exercise of power. However, the visible exercise of power is coupled with rendering invisible those people who are deemed "wrong", "bad" or "abnormal". They are excluded from the public arena and interned in prisons, asylums and psychiatric hospitals. This visible exertion of power makes resistance possible.

Foucault was also very politically involved. For example, he co-founded a grassroots organization for current and former prisoners and their relatives. He also acted as a journalist and a critical commentator on topical issues, for example the techniques of power and control applied in the health care system, the use of force in psychiatric institutions, and the societal repression of homosexuals (Heede, 2004).

Foucault claims that *modern power* has developed in the shadows of traditional power over the past 300 years, and that it has by now become the prevailing way of exercising social control. We should mention here that Foucault sticks to historical analyses of Western culture. Here, people are engaged in evaluating themselves – not morally but in relation to culturally and socially generated quantifiable norms. Actions are evaluated in relation to formal or informal scales of adequacy, competence, skill, efficiency, etc. Modern power is increasingly replacing some of the forms of traditional power.

Modern power is characterized by engaging people in activities that require them to monitor, scrutinize, evaluate and control the way they live their lives in relation to cultural norms. The exercise of power is invisible and subtle and hard to put a finger on. Nevertheless that is what Foucault attempts to do in his exploration of the *micro-physics* of power. While the exercise of power is invisible, indirect and subtle, the spotlight is directed at the life of the individual. Thus, the individual is exposed, put on display and publicly evaluated. How does this happen? It happens by means of a large number of new technologies that contain descriptions of normality/abnormality, performance tables and scales for rating many aspects of human behavior. According to Foucault, the disciplines of psychiatry, psychology, criminology and social work have played a crucial role in the development of the practices that underpin modern power.

Can the development of methods for management development, HR policies and organizational development be viewed as similar technologies: technologies that underpin the normalizing judgment of the individual manager or employee? We will return to this question later.

In 1983 Foucault wrote an Afterword to Michael Foucault. Beyond structuralism and hermeneutics, by Dreyfus and Rabinow. He opens with a question: Why study power? He offers the following answer: *"The ideas which I would like to discuss here represent neither a theory nor a methodology. I would like to say, first of all, what has been the goal of my work during the last twenty years. It has not been to analyze the phenomena of power, nor to elaborate the foundations of such an analysis. My objective, instead, has been to create a history of the different modes by which, in our culture, human beings are made subjects"* (Foucault, 1983, p. 208). He adds that it is not power, but the subject that constitutes the general theme in his endeavor.

Foucault rejected the ideal of objective knowledge that stems from the age of enlightenment. To him, all knowledge is historically and culturally contextual – including knowledge about mankind. In *The order of things: An archaeology of the human sciences* (1970), he wrote, *"man is only a recent invention"* – and an invention that may well be undergoing change in the future. In the following sections we discuss Foucault's ideas on how modern-day individuals are shaped as objects and subjects.

DISCIPLINARY TECHNOLOGIES

In Foucault's view modern man - as object and subject - is a historical product shaped by our views. The modern individual is the object of knowledge produced within the human sciences, and at the same time, is also a perceiving subject. Formative processes associated with power shape people as subjects and objects. Foucault described the dual role of the individual as follows: *"To sum up, [my] main objective ... is not so much to attack 'such or such' an institution of power, or group, or elite, or class, but rather a technique, a form of power. This form of power applies itself to immediate everyday life which categorizes the individual, marks him by his own individuality, attaches him to his own identity, imposes a law of truth on him which he must recognize and which others have to recognize in him. It is a form of power which makes individuals subjects. There are two meanings of the word subject: subject to someone else by control and dependence, and tied to his own identity by a conscience or self-knowledge. Both meanings suggest a form of power which subjugates and makes subject"* (Foucault, 1983, p. 212).

First we will examine how an individual is made into an object. This occurs by means of a wide range of disciplinary technologies (i.e. methods or processes) aimed at the individual's body and soul. Individuals are not disciplined through lectures or brute force but through procedures for training, categorization and sorting individuals. The disciplining power works through controlling observation and normalizing judgment, which is combined in the examination and testing of the individual (Dreyfus & Rabinow, 1983). The word "examination" reflects the duality of a process where the individual is both made the object of an examination and required to pass an "exam". The results of the examination enter into the normalizing judgment that determines a person's normative worth, that is, the person's scores on a wide range of scales. For example, the range of HR tools that – in Foucault's terminology – frame normalizing judgment is growing.

The objective of the controlling observation is to integrate surveillance into all types of production and control. Foucault offered scrupulous descriptions of the forms of surveillance that have been exercised at various times in history.

Previously, surveillance was closely associated with architecture, spatial design and the placement of individuals, for example in military camps, prisons, schools and housing units. The clearest example of the importance of spatial design in relation to surveillance is Jeremy Bentham's ideal model for an institution: the panopticon. Bentham was a philosopher and a social reformer who lived from 1748 to 1832. As a lawyer he wanted to reform an impenetrable legal system and abolish its brutal methods of punishment. He developed a utilitarian moral philosophy to form the basis for a reform of the judicial system. In 1791 he wrote the book *"Panopticon or the Inspection House"*, which described an architectural plan for a more humane design of prisons and institutions. The inmates would be placed in a circular structure of cells that could be observed from a tower situated in the center of the circle. Foucault claimed that the fundamental ideas behind the panopticon have been preserved in institutional architecture ever since. The panopticon was presented as *"an architectural stroke of genius that allows subjectification and effective control at minimal costs (for example the number of guards can be reduced to a very small number) and without any direct forms of physical violence"* (Heede, 2000, p. 99; translated for this edition).

Foucault was particularly interested in institutions where inmates were forced to spend all their time and often indefinitely: prisons, military camps, insane asylums. Here the reader might object that the physical design of total institutions has little to do with contemporary organizations. Let us offer a few examples that there are still some remnants in place. In many schools built in Denmark until the 1950s the individual classroom had a door with a peephole for the principal to check on the teacher and the students. The physical design of the hole meant that the teacher and the students could not tell whether the principal was looking in. A familiar example from life in organizations is the open-plan office. In the early 1990s the trend was to design large shared office spaces without individual cubicles. In many cases, this change did not go down without a fight. There were many objections from employees arguing that this arrangement created an unpleasant sense of being under constant surveillance. If Foucault had lived he would probably have thought the open-plan office a cunning design, as it made surveillance even more discreet. Instead of the manager watching the employees, the coworkers now watch each other. In the years since then, we have become so used to the physical design of open-plan offices that many of us no longer notice the surveillance aspect.

Another everyday example from life in organizations is the control potential offered by e-mail and mobile phones that have become natural features along with the introduction of flexible work schedules and work-from-home arrangements. This technology lets the manager monitor the staff's work efforts through the time stamps on e-mails and mobile phone calls.

Despite the similarities, there are also major differences between total institutions and modern organizations, as managers and employees now have far more flexible work schedules, a development that restricts the possibility of surveillance or requires new methods. At any rate, it is not possible to monitor managers and employees around the clock - except in connection with, for example, outdoor teambuilding courses, which many see as a sophisticated way for managers and employees to work on their personal development. These teambuilding courses function as temporary total institutions where the "inmates" are required to be together around the clock and sometimes even within an indefinite timeframe. Thus, it establishes a new framework for surveillance, observation, examination, and testing. The examination methods are discreet and implicit in the sense that the participating managers and employees are not aware what they will be exposed to, what they will be evaluated on, and how these findings will later be used within the organization. The disciplining power lurks behind the mantra of self-actualization or the obligation to undergo personal development (Groes & Haslebo, 2005).

Foucault used the panopticon as a metaphor for the disciplinary aspect of modern power: *"Foucault compares the new disciplinary formation of society with a generalized prison. However, he emphasizes that disciplining cannot be reduced simply to a negative and destructive force. It is highly productive. It not only produces the criminal as a new category of person but also the obedient military person, the useful worker and the schooled and educated child. The objective of this disciplinary technology, regardless of its institutional moorings, is to shape compliant bodies; useful individuals who can be used, changed and developed"* (Lindgren, 1997, p. 321; translated for this edition). Modern disciplining takes place anonymously, discreetly, without bloodshed, efficiently and without major expenses for surveillance.

Modern power is also sophisticated because of the invisibility of the controlling observation, examination and normalizing judgment. It is difficult to determine when one is the object of surveillance and examination. That makes it the safe option to police oneself, evaluate oneself and work on one's own development. Personal development and the disciplining of the body become an individual responsibility and a life-long project. Managers and employees to a large extent take this task upon themselves and thus become more or less willing participants in the disciplining and surveillance of their own lives. This is illustrated in the following story from a manager who willingly took part in an HR activity that can be characterized as an example of a normalizing judgment. It was a follow-up talk after a 360-degree appraisal, where the manager had been rated on several scales by himself and others.

When the results were in, the manager was offered external coaching – a setup that is becoming quite common in large public and private sector organizations. He showed up for the first coaching sessions with the results in the form of a seven-page document that contained both his own evaluation, the other respondents' evaluations, and a development plan. In this case there were 11 other organizational members, selected by the manager in question: members of his staff, his boss, and his management colleagues. Replies were anonymous. The survey included questions about ten competences, which were rated on nine-point scales, where 9 represented "considerable" and 1 "limited" competence in the area in question such as the ability to motivate employees, resolve conflicts, communicate, etc. In addition to the numerical assessment, the respondents were also able to offer three pieces of advice. Let's call the manager Steve. He was 50 years old and had been a manager for a number of years.

STORY 8: THE MANAGER WITH POOR RESULTS ON A 360-DEGREE APPRAISAL

Somewhat into the conversation we looked at the written report. Steve said that he had been very surprised by the results. In some areas there was a big difference between his own assessment and the average of the others' assessment. For example, he had given himself an 8 on communication, while the average for the other respondents was 3. On the ability to motivate his employees he had put down 7, while the average was only 4. He had studied the figures for the individual respondents carefully and tried to figure out who had given which rating. One respondent had assessed him as very ambitious and a very poor communicator — who might that be? Someone else had given him a rock-bottom rating for ambition and a top rating for organizational awareness - who might that be? Some of the advice was not only surprising, but had hurt him deeply. Someone had suggested that he be friendlier to people who were critical of him. He felt that he was a friendly person, but of course a manager was not supposed to just sit there and accept any old thing.

Someone else had written that he should stop making mountains out of molehills. Well, what did that mean? He saw himself as a results-oriented manager who made careful prioritizations. When he first read the report his initial thought was, "Do I even want to be a manager any longer? Maybe it's time I started looking for a new job."

The first night after he had received the report he found it virtually impossible to sleep. He was tossing and turning, wondering who had written what. The next day he had a scheduled meeting in the HR department where an HR consultant was going to go over the report with him. He had expressed his surprise at the results, but did not feel like revealing how hurt he felt. He had also said that he did not know what to do. He found it especially hard to deal with the assessment of him as a poor communicator. The HR consultant had suggested that he see an external consultant who could help him work on his personal communication style. He had accepted the offer, thinking that maybe he could get some input for his career concerns. Maybe he was not really cut out to be a manager? How could he face his employees when he did not know who had written what? Should he look for another job?

A little later during the first session the coach asked Steve if he would like to have some of the replies and the advice explained. No, definitely not, he replied – since he did not know whom to ask what. The whole thing would only become even more embarrassing.

It is clear that Steve's options for working on his personal development have not improved. The individual results have been removed from the specific contexts and relationships they refer to, and they make no sense to Steve. It also seems that the relationship between Steve and his employees has suffered, and that communication is now more difficult. What might happen when it is time for next year's 360-degree appraisal? This development instrument is expected to allow managers to compare two sets of results to see whether there is any progress. In Steve's case, by the next year two members of his staff had left, and three new members had joined. Since the replies were anonymous he had no idea which of the old evaluations to compare with the new ones. Now he had two sets of evaluations and still no clue.

How might Foucault's ideas about the shaping of the individual as an object shed light on this story? In Foucault's terminology, a 360-degree appraisal is a self-technology that is used as an instrument in a judgment. In companies, however, it is used as a development tool where the judgment aspect is formally toned down. Steve – and everybody else who has to undergo a traditional 360-degree appraisal – has no influence on the dimensions that they are being evaluated on. The forms are designed by experts, and for those involved they have an air of truth and scientific fact. This way of describing a manager appears scientific, and the image that emerges of Steve as a manager takes on the character of truth.

Although Steve did not recognize himself on several aspects of his employees' evaluations of him, he was unable to produce the idea that maybe a manager could be described in very different ways, or that maybe he should not accept this evaluation. The disciplining power is subtle and discreet and very hard to protest against. Steve, who was trained in natural science, was not in a position to cast doubt about the psychological methods of description.

Conducting a traditional 360-degree appraisal in an organization is a lengthy process: First, there is information for the respondents according to instructions from the HR department. Then the respondents complete the questionnaire. Next, the HR department analyzes the results, and the reports are sent to the individual managers. He or she then reflects on the results and holds a department meeting to discuss the results. Throughout this process Steve was trapped in the obvious logic of the self-technology, which offered no possible means of escape for him. During the first coaching session, he could only place his feeling of humiliation and diminished self-esteem within himself. This experience gave rise to desperate soul-searching about whether he should just give up being a manager. Steve was cast as an inept manager, and his possibilities of coordinating his actions with the employees were reduced.

If we compare Steve's experience of being humiliated with Honneth's concepts discussed in Chapter 6, we can construe these events as a violation of Steve's social value as a contributor to the cooperation within his department. An injury that is not the result of anything said by his employees in the follow-up meeting or likely to be what the employees intended. The story does not reveal how the employees felt about the whole thing, what they discussed among themselves, or what options they envisioned for themselves at the meeting where the manager's feedback and action plan were to be discussed. A qualified guess would be that many experienced it as an awkward situation where it was hard for them to say anything at all since they could not – in an extension of the anonymity of the process – say what they had put in the questionnaire.

Why is the result a moral humiliation when the objective was to promote development? To answer this question we need to incorporate the concept of context and the moral obligation to strive for creating clear contexts (see

Chapter 3). A 360-degree appraisal combines an evaluation context with a development context. The two contexts are governed by very different rules. An evaluation context generates subject-object relationships, while a development context generates subject-subject relationships. Here, the previously quoted observation by Peter Lang is relevant again: *"When the context is unclear, you invite craziness into the room"*. Seen through this lens, traditional management evaluations with the declared intention of promoting the manager's personal development can be viewed as a systematized framework of degradation of the organizational member's social value to the work community.

This does not imply that evaluation is never useful; if the context is clear for both parties, for example, a recruitment process, and the procedures and aims are well-explained, evaluation may be necessary and meaningful. If it is clearly a context of evaluation and decision making, aims and methods designed to facilitate personal development should be excluded. It can be a very frustrating and demeaning experience for the candidate to participate in a job interview that suddenly changes into a developmental or therapeutic conversation.

CONFESSION TECHNOLOGIES

As Foucault explained in his Afterword *Why study power?* his interest lay in a historical analysis of the modes of power in order to study how individuals have been made into objects throughout history (Foucault, 1983). With a similar purpose, Foucault also studied the history of sexuality to uncover how the individual has been shaped as a subject throughout history, although he did not make this point quite explicitly. Perhaps he did not do this because he passed away before volumes 2 and 3 of the history of sexuality had been completed.

As Foucault explained in his Afterword Why study power? his interest lay in a historical analysis of the modes of power in order to study how individuals have been made into objects throughout history (Foucault, 1983). With a similar purpose, Foucault also studied the history of sexuality to uncover how the individual has been shaped as a subject throughout history, although he did not make this point quite explicitly. Perhaps he did not do this because he passed away before volumes 2 and 3 of the history of sexuality had been completed.

Foucault traced various forms of confession technologies back through time – from the confession of sins in a religious setting to secular confessions in medical studies and psychiatric records to modern-day confessions of one's deepest thoughts and feelings featured on television's domestic dramas. The purpose was to explore the history of confession (Dreyfus & Rabinow, 1983). *"The confession has spread its effects far and wide. It plays a part in justice, medicine, education, family relationships and love relationships, in the most ordinary affairs of everyday life, and in the most solemn rites; one confesses one's crimes, one's sins, one's thoughts and desires, one's illnesses and troubles… One admits to oneself, in pleasure and pain, things it would be impossible to tell anyone else, the things people write books about… Western man has become a confessing animal"* (Foucault, 1980, p. 59). In the words of Nikolas Rose, whom we mentioned in Chapter 3: *"In compelling, persuading and inciting subjects to disclose themselves, finer and more intimate regions of personal and interpersonal life come under surveillance and are opened up for expert judgment, and normative evaluation, for classification and correction"* (Rose, 1999, p. 244).

Foucault explains how confession places individuals in a network of power relations with professionals who claim to be able to derive the truth from the confessions because they have access to important keys of interpretation. Confession is closely related to the demand in Western cultures for the individual to know the truth – the truth about him/herself. The scientific development within medical science, psychiatry and psychology has played an important role in linking confession, truth and power. The individual has been made the object of scientific descriptions and a subject who ought to tell the truth about him/herself in order to achieve improved self-insight.

Modern power is exercised in ways in which disciplining and the less visible confession technologies mutually enhance each other. The conviction that experts can help us learn the truth about ourselves has become so prevailing in Western culture that it is seen as natural and taken for granted. One consequence of this thinking is the notion that if only the individual breaks free from oppressive power, the truth about the individual will emerge. Currently, this mindset is reflected in the forms of coaching that are based on realism and focused on the individual as an autonomous entity that needs to break free from inner and outer restrictions of personal self-expression. Foucault did not, however, view modern power as oppressive but as productive: The individual's self-image is shaped by the historically and culturally generated modern power. There is no universal truth about man and no inner truth to set free.

Foucault argued that the interpretative sciences that are interested in meaning, and that continue to search for "deep" truths about the human psyche, practice an art of interpretation that promotes suspicion. According to this viewpoint, the neutral scientist has privileged access to defining meaning and truth, while the persons making the confessions and revealing his or her secrets are not capable of interpreting them. Foucault claimed that it is an illusion to search for a deeper truth underneath the surface phenomena based on the notion that the goal is to discover what is "really" going on. *"The hermeneutics of suspicion rightly has the uneasy suspicion that it has not been suspicious enough"* (Dreyfus & Rabinow, 1983, p. 181).

Let us return to the story about Steve and the incomprehensible 360-degree appraisal. As mentioned, the process in a traditional 360-degree appraisal proceeds in phases. In Foucault's terminology we might describe these phases as follows: first the shaping of the manager as an object and then the confession. When the 360-degree appraisal is used in organizations, it is rarely explicitly stated that the majority is right. Nevertheless, discussions of disagreements between the employees' feedback and the manager's self-evaluation are based on two key assumptions. Firstly, that it is possible to draw a clear-cut and truthful image of a manager. Thus, the employees' and the manager's assessments should ideally be in agreement. Otherwise, the employees are right, and the manager is under suspicion of presenting an overly rosy picture or simply lacking self-insight.

The second assumption is that it is the points of disagreement that are interesting. Hence, the manager should be willing to receive feedback especially in the areas where the employees have a more negative view than his own. Not only must he accept that the employees' assessment represents the truth; he also has to offer confessions about what he "now" sees as the error of his ways. Failing to offer a confession is not an option. Or, to put it differently, managers who do not accept the evaluations and offer a confession will either have demonstrated that they are not willing to work on their personal development or that they are completely entrenched in their self-conception. The latter is a dangerous path that will undermine any hopes of career development.

Steve found it very difficult even to talk to the employees about the results. He only saw what he could not do: He could not tell them how surprised he was. He could not tell them how hurt he felt and he could definitely not tell them that he was considering pulling out of management. He also could not ask the employees what lay behind their evaluations since they were made in anonymity. His only option was to say that he *understood* what they were saying, and that he would strive to improve. On this basis, Steve is now obligated to work on his personal development plan. If he finds this difficult he can accept the offer of external coaching.

The confession of sins or the admission of mistakes is practiced in many forms of organizational development. The story about Steve exemplifies a systematized approach with the declared aim of promoting individual development. There are other approaches with the declared aim of generating joint learning or development of the work community, for example with regard to teamwork, commitment and professional pride. Often, this takes place in two-day retreats for managers and employees from the same organization with the assistance of external consultants. Many of the methods have their roots in the discourse on the necessity of personal development. The question remains, however, whether it is possible to achieve shared understanding and coordination of meaning and action with methods that have an individual focus? Would a seminar with 20 participants ever accomplish more than simply individual development times 20?

An example of a method used at retreats and seminars is a three-phase process. In Phase One, the consultant highlights typical errors and sins committed in relation to the theme of the seminar. If the theme is teamwork, for example, errors and sins may include *keeping knowledge to oneself, gossiping, being late for meetings, not keeping one's promises,* etc. In Phase Two, the individual participants admit their sins and errors: Which of these examples do they recognize from their own behavior? This can take place discreetly, or the individual participant may confess in front of the entire group. Phase Three is about repentance: How can the individual participant refrain from committing similar mistakes in the future? This phase may involve the consultant doing an interview with individual participants in front of the group about why he or she makes the mistake, how often it happens, who is an accomplice, which personal benefits it offers, and when he or she will stop doing it. This phase is often completed with an individual assignment of drafting a personal development plan, which may be made public. Thus, the three phases are about identifying errors and sins, admitting one's own mistakes and sins, and individually pledging to improve.

Many participants in these seminars weigh their options as events unfold. They are very uncertain as to whether they are allowed to turn down an exercise, whether they can go home at night or leave the seminar altogether. Many of these thoughts and the doubts they represent spring from the limited amount of information that is offered beforehand. Typically, the information is limited to an abstract objective and a time and a place. Thus, there is no information about the concrete activities, methods or theoretical underpinnings of the seminar. Without this information it is impossible to know what one agrees to by taking part – and similarly impossible to know whether there are elements that one might want to be able to turn down. One of the most fundamental ethical guidelines in professional development work is the principle of *informed consent*. Without the information we have just mentioned, the participants can in principle only offer *blind consent*. An effect of blind consent is often that the participants are only physically present while mentally distancing themselves from the unfolding events in an effort to protect themselves and preserve their self-esteem and self-respect. This survival strategy requires a great deal of energy, and active participation and learning are consequently pushed to the background.

This survival strategy is necessary when we do not feel that we have a real choice: Staying on and taking part might require personal compromises, but opting out and leaving prematurely may carry even worse repercussions. There is a risk of stigmatization, being labeled as "walled up", "not willing to share", "too insecure to see it through" or "resisting change". None of the options that present themselves are attractive, as they may carry unacceptable consequences. The result may be a form of paralysis, so that the person sees the seminar through while concentrating on limiting the damage.

How can experiences of loss of face and of having no real options occur, when the stated goal by the organization is enhanced teamwork, team spirit, job satisfaction, etc.? We think the answer lies in the assumptions about change and development that these seminars rest on. The discourse on the necessity of personal development obligates the participants to look within themselves, face the truth about themselves and be prepared to work on their so called blind spots and weak sides. In Foucault's terminology, this is a *confession technology*. If we view confession as a discourse and consider how the participants are positioned we see that they are collectively positioned as sinners, while the managers often act as observers and thus may escape this positioning. Who is positioned as the pastor that offers absolution varies from case to case. In some cases it is the consultant; in other cases it is management. Underlying the confession rationale is an implicit assumption that once someone has confessed a sin the person will strive to improve, which will enhance their ability and motivation to work and cooperate. However, the effects are often the opposite: Experiences involving loss of face and blind consent diminish the desire to share personal experiences and concerns with one's colleagues. It is often the case that the events of the seminar remain detached from everyday life of the organization. People simply do not feel like talking about what happened.

The intentions of such programs are good but are highly unlikely to lead to improved possibilities of action in the form of improved teamwork, team spirit, job satisfaction, etc.

RESISTING MODERN SELF-TECHNOLOGIES

Foucault has been criticized for placing too much emphasis on the submission and disciplining of the individual and on the external control, compliance and passiveness of the subject. Is it not possible to offer resistance to modern power? In Story 8: *The Manager with poor Results on a 360-Degree Appraisal* we saw that resistance is not easy. We will now look at another story in which the main character unexpectedly wound up in trouble.

The events took place in a large private company, which makes consistent use of well-defined concepts concerning management development, pre-management training, staff satisfaction surveys, customer satisfaction surveys, annual staff performance and development reviews, annual management appraisals, etc. The following story was told as part of a long-term coaching process a few years ago. The story is told by Jon, who is a specialist and has been with the company for seven years. The events in question had occurred one year earlier.

STORY 9: THE EMPLOYEE WHO INADVERTENTLY BETRAYED A FRIEND

It's time again for the annual survey of staff satisfaction, and I'm in a fix. When we did the same survey last year, things did not go well. Jim and I were not keen to complete the questionnaire, although we would have liked to express our criticism of our supervisor, Martin, who we both think has a very bureaucratic and authoritarian management style. Martin has been the boss for two years, and before then we had a very qualified supervisor who was not so hung up on paperwork and control. Jim and I are probably the most critical – at least judging by what is said in our department meetings.

Jim and I discussed what would happen if we didn't fill out the question-naire. Would the HR department be able to trace who had completed it, and who hadn't? What would happen if we handed it in, and ours were the most critical? How would Martin react? Could we really be sure that the replies were anonymous? We had a lot of doubts.

So I decided to talk to one of our in-house HR consultants that I'm on good terms with. That was a big step to take. Informally, the in-house HR consultants are referred to as our "in-house intelligence service". But Sophie is okay, I think, and we had a fine talk. Sophie assured me there was nothing to worry about. There would be no way to identify my questionnaire. But since the deadline was really close, I decided not to fill it out after all.

Then the survey was carried out, and the results were analyzed. Each department had its own report. In my department there is a staff of twelve. The report included graphic presentations of the answers to each of the questions. In all the diagrams there was one reply that stood out as far more negative than the rest. I don't think anyone could see whether it was the same person or different persons who had given the critical feedback. That led to a lot of guesswork among the employees.

A few weeks later it was time for the annual staff performance and development reviews. I was not looking forward to that. The meeting began okay, though. Martin asked some questions about my job tasks, and there are no problems there. But then Martin pulled out the report and asked me what I thought about it. It was hard to have anything to say about that. Then Martin turned to some of the questions that had very critical feedback and asked if those were my replies. I was treading water and managed to say that it was supposed to be anonymous. But Martin kept asking about specific replies. At some point I was so provoked that the words just flew out of my mouth: *"I never even completed that questionnaire!"*

Then the room was quiet. For a long time. Martin shuffled his papers around, looked down, looked up, and then said, *"All right, then I guess all the critical replies are Jim's!"*

The rest of the meeting was under a cloud. There was only one thought on my mind: What am I going to say to Jim? Afterwards I had very mixed feelings. I felt really guilty toward Jim, and I wanted to do something to keep him out of any future trouble. I was also angry with Martin: Surely it wasn't fair or reasonable to be subjected to a third-degree about an anonymous survey? I was also angry with myself because I hadn't been able to see that if I spoke up, the arrow would have to be pointing at Jim. I hadn't seen that in the situation. And now it's that time of year again. The deadline for the survey is this Friday. What do I do?

While Story 8 was about a manager who saw no way of escaping a management appraisal, in Story 9 it is an employee required to give (not receive) feedback who is in a fix. While Steve did not mention any considerations about what he might do to escape the situation, Jon has carefully considered his options and the possible consequences. Although he eventually decided not to take part, he did not get away with it but wound up with a big and unexpected ethical problem that was about potentially having harmed a close colleague. In both stories we see that not only modern power but also traditional power is at play. Management and staff functions exercise centralized control that is both oppressive and restricting. Forms of repressive and modern power are entangled in each other in the ways that HR activities are carried out.

Foucault offers several interesting observations on the possibilities for offering resistance in the Afterword to *Why Study Power?* (Foucault, 1983). Here he speaks about the fights that are worth fighting, such as the fight *against the control that promotes individualization*. It is also worth fighting against the knowledge regimens that define the truth about who we are: *"But the task of philosophy as a critical analysis of our world is something which is more and more important. Maybe the most certain of all philosophical problems is the problem of the present time, and of what we are, in this very moment. Maybe the target nowadays is not to discover what we are, but to refuse what we are. We have to imagine and to build up what we could be to get rid of this kind of political 'double bind', which is the simultaneous individualization and totalization of modern power structures. The conclusion would be that the political, ethical, social, philosophical problem of ours days is not to try to liberate us both from the state and from the type of individualization which is linked to the state. We have to promote new forms of subjectivity through the refusal of this kind of individuality which has been imposed on us for several centuries"* (Foucault, 1983, p. 216).

The Australian psychologist Michael White has made an important contribution to the development of a more optimistic application of Foucault's ideas in a therapeutic setting. He has crucially expanded the tiny cracks of possibility of escaping the modern power that Foucault only hints at. In his article *Addressing Personal Failure* White claims that there has been a significant growth in the phenomenon of *personal failure* in recent decades (White, 2002). He bases this claim on his years of experience as a therapist: many of the psychological problems he encounters are about experiences of personal inadequacy, incompetence, shortcomings, defeat and the inability to create a life that is in accordance with our cultural norms. White has developed a very constructive way of addressing these experiences in therapy, and he offers a highly interesting analysis of the links between the widespread experiences of personal defeat and the modern power systems, which owe much to Foucault.

According to Foucault people are recruited into oppressing and disciplining themselves as described earlier in this chapter. This observation draws a bleak picture of the individual's capacity for self-determination. But that is unfounded, says White. It is possible to use Foucault's ideas in more uplifting ways.

First, an analysis of the workings of modern power must also enable a discovery of examples of situations where people refuse to accept certain versions of culturally determined norms. It should be noted here that White, whose thinking is rooted in post-structuralism, does not see the individual as existing outside the culture or in opposition to it but as shaped within the culture. Western culture, however, offers a wide diversity of discourses, narratives, norms and values that the individual can relate to and address.

Second, the professional disciplines of psychology, psychiatry, etc. that have contributed to the development of the technologies of modern power can also contribute to the development of methods that expand people's opportunities of resisting, rejecting or indeed transforming the ways in which modern power defines our identity, relationships and ways of living: White uses these ideas as a springboard for developing methods and questions in his therapeutic practice that invite the client to focus on and articulate activities and actions which help shape his or her self-conception, relationships and way of living.

White reviews the ways in which personal failure and modern forms of power are related. These failures fall into three categories: lapses, omissions and resistances. Here, we will only mention a few examples of each. *Lapses* may involve a failure to achieve desired ends with regard to personal development objectives or simple mistakes and errors of everyday life that others view as a lack of social competence. *Omissions* may involve overlooking opportunities to realize one's full potential or to rank self and/or others on widely accepted tables of performance. Both lapses and omissions can be hard to notice in the flow of everyday events. *Resistances*, however, are more visible. They may involve an obstinate rejection of aspirations to achieve superior status in an organization or a headstrong refusal to pursue self-actualization.

White reviews the ways in which personal failure and modern forms of power are related. These failures fall into three categories: lapses, omissions and resistances. Here, we will only mention a few examples of each. Lapses may involve a failure to achieve desired ends with regard to personal development objectives or simple mistakes and errors of everyday life that others view as a lack of social competence. Omissions may involve overlooking opportunities to realize one's full potential or to rank self and/or others on widely accepted tables of performance. Both lapses and omissions can be hard to notice in the flow of everyday events. Resistances, however, are more visible. They may involve an obstinate rejection of aspirations to achieve superior status in an organization or a headstrong refusal to pursue self-actualization.

White makes the intriguing point that all three forms of personal failure can be perceived as attempts to escape normalizing judgment. When a person talks about his or her experiences of being assigned an identity by others that the person does not accept, the objection will often be expressed within the framework of our culture: for example, "My boss says that I'm not assertive enough, but I don't want to be the sort of person that just walks all over other people". We do not see it as appropriate or useful for a therapist or a consultant to ask questions that are based on the rationale of normalizing judgment and thus focus on disagreements between the description of the person and existing cultural norms. Questions such as, "Why aren't you more assertive?", "What does your boss mean by 'your personal assertiveness'?", "What do you understand by 'your personal assertiveness'?" or "What can you do to make your boss notice your assertiveness more?" might lead to new interesting thoughts, but they also risk keeping the conversation on a narrow track. Furthermore, they risk locking the person into a conviction that "assertiveness" represents a universal ideal for human nature.

THE OBLIGATION TO INTERACT AS MORALLY RESPONSIBLE AGENTS

Managers and employees often have very unpleasant experiences associated with 360-degree appraisals or similar methods – even if they have accepted the demand for personal development and self-actualization. The opportunities for putting words to the unpleasant experiences are limited, as we described in our discussion of the stories in this chapter. In organizations it takes a great effort to create contexts that make it possible to challenge the fundamental assumptions underlying these applied self-technologies. In addition, the obligation to undergo personal development is associated with an individualist perspective, which strongly suggests that unpleasant experiences can be explained with references to individual characteristics: lack of competence, lack of personal strength and lack of confidence, as illustrated in Steve's story. We also encountered this dilemma in Story 4: *Trial Period Evaluation turned Therapy*, in which the narrator described how unpleasant it was to have to listen to the supervisor's feedback and directions for her personal development, and that the best she could do was to stay, listen and refuse to say anything.

It takes a special context to create an opportunity to put words to unpleasant experiences. External coaching can offer an opportunity – provided the coach is *not* also firmly embedded in the widespread individualist perspective with its emphasis on self-actualization and normalizing judgment. In that case the coach may simply intensify the modern power and exacerbate the situation.

Instead of staying within the framework of the normalizing judgment the coach may, however, choose a completely different basis for his or her questions. If a person fails to live up to well-established norms, it may be because the person wants to lead a different life and is engaged in alterna-tive identity-building projects that are very important to him or her. White offers this fascinating description: "*When people consult me about personal failure I routinely anticipate exciting expeditions into territories of identity that have been little charted. I also expect that these expeditions will provide people with the opportunity to step into modes of life and thought that will bring new horizons of possibility to their lives*" (White, 2003, p. 42).

One way of moving on would be to explore what enabled the "personal failure" in the sense of an objection to the normalizing judgment. Questions that invite reflection might be, "How did you reach the conclusion that this is not something you want to do?", "How do you wish to position yourself as a manager and organizational member?", "What sorts of interactions with others would you like to initiate?", "Which relationships would help to make this possible?". Questions in this vein can lead to a richer description of the "personal failure" and its relational context. This approach focuses on the person's moral judgment and ethical reflections about the types of relation-ships he or she wishes to create. The person is reinstated as a morally respon-sible agent who acts with thoughtfulness and care, who possesses skills and competences and who assumes responsibility for his or her actions and their consequences for others and the organization as a whole.

REFLECTIONS

Foucault's thoughts on traditional and modern power and White's narrative therapeutic practice may provide inspiration for raising a number of impor-tant questions about the connection between power and morality in organi-zations.

Although Foucault claimed that modern power has become dominant at the cost of traditional power, we see both modes of power at play in organizations. Traditional power is evident in the centralized policies and concepts for management, employees and organizational development that are imposed from the top as mandatory requirements. For example, mandatory management appraisals, workplace environment assessments, and workplace climate surveys are built into many institutional performance contracts. Management and the individual HR department can hardly refuse this requirement – even if there is growing concern in many organizations about negative consequences of the methods that are applied as well as a growing desire to find new methods. The individual manager or employee has even less room to maneuver. As illustrated by many of our stories, organizational members are not only faced with the obligation to undergo personal development, but are also coerced into taking part in the scheduled development activities without receiving any information about the objective, methods and ground rules – and without knowing the consequences of opting out. In organizations, a choice is rarely explicitly defined, just as the consequences of taking part or opting out are also rarely put into words. Managers and employees therefore fear that refusing to take part will have a negative impact on their working conditions, pay conditions, income, and career opportunities.

Traditional power ensures the physical participation of managers and employees, but not necessarily their mental participation. As we saw both in Story 4: *Trial Period Evaluation turned Therapy* and Story 8: *The Manager with poor Results on a 360-Degree Appraisal*, the main characters struggle in their inner dialogue to distance themselves from the external events and preserve their self-respect and self-esteem. Both cases involve denial of rights and degradation (in Honneth's terminology), where the persons – despite the declared aim of development – feel that their moral integrity and personal dignity are compromised.

However, in many cases modern power also ensures mental participation. As we have discussed, modern power is invisible and subtle because it is built into the practices and self-technologies in use in organizations. To the extent that these take on a scientific form and are perceived as appropriate for defining the truth about someone, modern power and normalizing judgment make it extremely difficult to opt out. The ever growing repertoire of practices that frame normalizing judgments in organizations represents time-consuming activities that take time away from the job itself and shift the attention to the individual, who is given the task of introspection. Instead of activities where the individual managers and employees appraise themselves in relation to individual norms and scales, the focus might be directed, for example, at an appreciative inquiry into the events where organizational members were successful in coordinating the actions that are necessary for everybody to do a good job.

From our point of view, management, HR departments and consultants have a great responsibility for seeking new avenues in considering the methods and tools that recognize and appreciate the individual manager and employee both as morally responsible agents and as contributors to the work community. These methods should serve as a meeting place for managers and employees, who are all given a voice as morally responsible and reliable persons within mutually respectful relationships.

In our final chapter we gather the threads of this book and weave them into a new pattern to explore how social responsibility, the obligation to engage in dialogue, the shared responsibility for positioning, inquiry of value to the work community and the obligation to interact as morally responsible agents together make up the moral compass points in relational ethics.

CHAPTER 8

MORAL COMPASS POINTS
IN RELATIONAL ETHICS

We have traveled far and wide, and in this closing chapter we put the pieces together and offer a new understanding of the paths that may take us from good intentions to more and better possibilities of action as we face complex moral dilemmas in organizations.

First we want to add a few comments to the nine stories in this book, which have provided an invaluable source of inspiration for expanding our understanding of the complexity in everyday events in organizations, and which have challenged us in our attempts to find and develop approaches that can be useful in situations characterized by moral dilemmas and doubts.

In Chapter 2 we described some of the key assumptions in the social constructionist epistemology and argued that the choice of epistemology is also a choice of ethics. We illustrated how social constructionism is closely associated with relational ethics. Key concepts in this book: *context, relationship, discourse, appreciation* and *power* lead us to define a set of moral compass points, which can be illustrated as a flower with five petals: *social responsibility, the obligation to engage in dialogue, shared responsibility for positioning, inquiry of value to the work community* and the *obligation to interact as morally responsible agents.* Each of the petals can be unfolded further into a series of moral obligations and entitlements, based on summaries from previous chapters as well as some added detail.

Finally, we will pass the baton to others. In this book we have taken a few additional steps, but there are still many loose ends and topics that deserve much more attention than we have been able to give them in this book.

INSIGHTS FROM THE NINE STORIES

With our nine stories from real life in organizations we wanted to illustrate how all parties involved may have had good reasons to act the way they did, and that any event can be understood in a variety of ways and lead in many different directions. Each narrator is bound to relate the events from their particular position, and we have then provided various alternative angles and possible perspectives on the events. In many cases we have also speculated about the possible future directions events might take, depending on the actors' moral choices. The stories have been crucial to our efforts to develop useful concepts and to illustrate how all events and actions have ethical aspects.

It has struck us how the narrators, who have many ethical reflections about their possibilities of action, are mostly alone in these deliberations. Not only are moral dilemmas hard to put into words, it is also difficult to find situations in everyday life in organizations where one can discuss ethical concerns with a colleague or manager. That may be due to the time pressures of work or the sense that the topic is not strictly speaking a part of one's work content. Another possible reason may be a limited language for speaking about morality and ethics, or indeed a dangerous language that addresses moral dilemmas and doubts in an individualist perspective which focuses on personal inadequacies and invites the allocation of blame.

In most of the nine stories, the narrator either experienced a loss of face, a loss of personal dignity or a moral humiliation, or he or she is concerned about how to avoid or prevent a loss of dignity for him/herself or others. Some of the stories involve careful reflections on the opportunities of reestablishing dignity and repairing damaged relationships. In some cases the loss of face is so severe that the narrator's membership in the organization is threatened. This happens either because the narrator is excluded from work contexts (as in Story 2: *Friendly Concern or Sexual Harassment?*) or because the person considers resigning (as in Story 8: *The Manager with poor Results on a 360-Degree Appraisal*).

Another striking feature in many of the stories is that the main characters - and possibly some of the other characters as well – spend a great deal of time considering possibilities of action and contacting others to regain their dignity and reestablish important work relationships. It is our impression that a considerable amount of time is spent in this way, without anyone knowing.

RELATIONAL ETHICS AS A USEFUL GUIDE FOR MORAL CHOICES

In recent decades the prevailing ethical thinking has been influenced by *universalism* and *fundamentalism* (Bauman, 1993). *Universalism* describes universal ethical instructions that everyone must accept as valid. *Fundamentalism* is a power-based definition that makes it an absolute necessity to follow certain ethical instructions to retain one's membership of a given society or community.

In organizations too, a universalist and fundamentalist mindset has influenced many efforts to define a common basis for handling its moral dilemmas. The common basis may consist of ethical guidelines or principles that apply to a certain group of professionals (social workers, psychologists, etc.), in the establishment of a code for "good governance" that applies to municipal management or in the establishment of a set of values that applies to management and employees in a particular company. These efforts are based on the assumption that the members of an organization will know what to do in morally challenging situations if they have access to detailed guidelines and a firm, value-based foundation on which to rely. As we discussed in Chapter 4 in particular, general ethical guidelines are not enough to guide us to a moral choice in specific and unique situations. That is not a viable approach. Bauman makes this point even more clearly: *"The foolproof – universal and unshakably founded – ethical code will never be found; having singed our fingers once too often, we know now what we did not know then, when we embarked on this journey of exploration: that ..., an ethics that is universal and 'objectively founded' is a practical impossibility: perhaps also an oxymoron, a contradiction in terms"* (Bauman, 1993, p. 10).

Morally challenging situations can be understood in many different ways, and the moral quality of an action can be evaluated on the basis of many different and often contradictory and conflicting criteria. An ethical basis offers no guarantee for morally responsible actions:

"No logically coherent ethical code can 'fit' the essentially ambivalent condition of morality. Neither can rationality 'override' moral impulse: at the utmost, it can silence it and paralyze, thereby rendering the chances of the 'good being done' not stronger, perhaps weaker, than they otherwise would have been. What follows is that moral conduct cannot be guaranteed; not by better designed contexts for human action, nor by better formed motives of human action. We need to learn how to live without such guarantees, and with the awareness that guarantees will never be offered – that a perfect society, as well as a perfect human being, is not a viable prospect, while attempts to prove the contrary result in more cruelty than humanity, and certainly less morality" (Bauman, 1993, pp. 10-11).

It is similarly pointless in an organization to wait for the emergence of a perfect organizational culture, perfect management and perfect working conditions – as something that *others* should make available.

If we do not have a firm moral basis to stand on and also cannot wait for others to deliver optimum conditions – what can we do? What do we do when universal theories offer little help and we have to make moral choices in specific situations? One possibility would be to rely on our intuition and gut feeling about right and wrong. The discourse on personal development in the sense of an actualization of the individual's authentic inner core can lead to a subjectivist moral philosophy where individual intuitions are seen as valid and strong arguments for moral choices. This possibility too we have to reject as inadequate, as did many of our narrators; they refused to be satisfied by vague feelings and sensations or by good intentions and instead looked for more convincing arguments for their moral choices.

Thus, in our search for reasons for moral choices we can either look for universal principles *outside* the individual or for signals *within* the individual – or we can choose a third path where we take an interest in what goes on *among* people in the relationships we create through language and communication. It is this third path we chose in Chapter 2 when we took the leap to social constructionism and relational ethics.

Thus, relational ethics constitutes a third path. We will now take a closer look at the five moral compass points in relational ethics.

KEY CONCEPTS AND MORAL COMPASS POINTS

As we have demonstrated in previous chapters, reflections on each of the selected social constructionist key terms leads to moral obligations. In

Chapter 2 we discussed how the epistemology of social constructionism is closely associated with relational ethics whereby the moral quality of an action is assessed on the extent to which it helps to strengthen the mutual relatedness in the organization and to improve the conditions of the work community. In Figure 1 we presented our understanding of the key terms that are particularly useful as a basis for handling moral dilemmas in organizations and demonstrated how these concepts interact. We will now combine these concepts and the associated moral compass points into the flower that illustrates relational ethics.

Figure 13: Key Concepts and Moral Compass Points in Relational Ethics

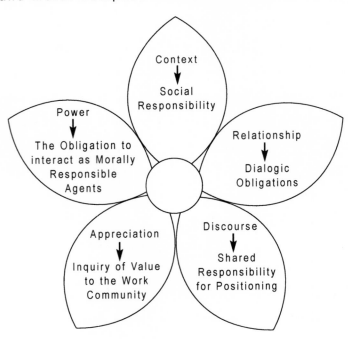

Each petal constitutes a moral compass point that serves as a headline. This headline may guide ethical reflections in complex everyday situations that do not present any obvious possibilities of action acceptable to the persons involved. Firstly, the moral compass points can be used in unnoticed and seemingly trivial everyday events to help us coordinate our own actions with those of others in flexible and creative ways that help us move toward a desirable future. Secondly, they can be used in more dramatic situations where the moral choice at a bifurcation point can be of crucial importance for future events and for the understanding of previous events.

A moral compass point is quite different from a set of rules. Adhering to a rule akin to "red means stop; green means go" does not require much reflection. By contrast, at a moral compass point we need to pause and think out actions that best fit the situation in question, and which are most likely to help build a desirable future for everyone involved. A rule demands that the person adjusts, while a moral compass point requires an active and responsible effort that includes reflection, social creativity, and judgment. In the next section we examine the moral obligations and entitlements implied by each of the five compass points.

OBLIGATIONS AND ENTITLEMENTS IN RELATIONAL ETHICS

In previous chapters we have emphasized obligations. The word obligation is chosen carefully, as it refers to a responsibility or task that a person chooses to take on, and which exceeds requirements in legislation, employment contracts and other formal documents. Obligations are about the informal and unwritten "rules" for what constitutes good behavior in relation to others. We have focused less on entitlements, although obligations and entitlements are inextricably linked. When colleagues feel obligated to talk to everybody in the department, everyone similarly is entitled to be included in the formal and informal conversations that take place. Entitlements are about justifiable expectations about what others should or should not do to you.

Some relationships, such as collegial relationships, are characterized by symmetrical codes of conduct: Both parties must live up to the same obligations and can expect to be treated accordingly. One person's obligation is the other person's entitlement. Other relationships are characterized by asymmetrical codes of conduct. For example, a doctor can give directions to a nurse, while the opposite is rarely the case. Here, the parties have different moral obligations and entitlements.

Although we have not addressed formally defined rights and duties in organizations, they also are of interest because it is often unclear whether there are any formal rules for certain choices and actions. In most organizations, for example, it is unclear whether the formal rights assigned to management include the right to demand that every employee take part in an outdoor teambuilding activity. This activity might require them to participate around the clock (regardless of legislation or formal agreements about maximum work hours), engage in unfamiliar tasks with unknown objectives and are unable to contact their families during the activity. We have only been able to touch very briefly on these grey areas and hope that others will address them in depth.

We have focused on moral obligations and entitlements that are informal and unwritten. For more than a century, interest organizations have negotiated formally defined rights and duties; trade unions in particular have aimed at protecting the entitlements and rights of employees, but have had little to say about their obligations. In this book we have set out to shed new light on the symmetrical and asymmetrical obligations and entitlements of managers, consultants and employees – with an emphasis on obligations.

Our objective has been to arrive at specific moral obligations and entitlements in relational ethics. When organizational members live up to and adhere to relational ethics, what then, are they aspiring to do? How would everyday interactions play out? How would managers and employees relate to each other? How would consultants make themselves useful to managers and employees? How would employees talk to and about customers, clients, citizens, patients, students, etc.?

We offer answers to these questions in the table below by unfolding each petal of the flower in Figure 13. As a petal unfolds, we further specify the obligations and entitlements that are associated with that particular moral compass point, based both on a summary of the points we have made earlier and on additional elaboration. To underline that the moral obligations are joint efforts we have used the terms "we" and "us".

Figure 14: Moral Obligations
and Entitlements in Relational Ethics

SOCIAL RESPONSIBILITY

1. We assume and exercise responsibility for the way our communication might attribute meaning to interactions in the past, present and future.

2. We assume and exercise responsibility for our own contributions to the creation of desirable speech acts.

3. We assume and exercise responsibility for the punctuation of series of events – well aware that the choice of "when it all began" creates meaning.

4. We assume and exercise responsibility for the way in which our speech acts influence the plot in a story.

5. We assume and exercise responsibility for making moral choices at bifurcation points in conversations.

6. We assume and exercise responsibility for creating clear and shared contexts.

DIALOGIC OBLIGATIONS

1. We speak with others rather than about others who are not present. If we have to speak about others we do it in a way that they would be pleased to listen if they were present.

2. We focus more on the multitude of meaning-constructing processes and patterns of communication than on making moral judgments of individual actions.

3. We move within the field of tension between exposing ourselves to others' points of view and preserving our own moral point of view – especially in situations that are characterized by major differences and disagreement.

4. We stimulate our own and others' curiosity and learning by asking open-ended and explorative questions.

5. We use language in ways that build mutually respectful relationships.

SHARED RESPONSIBILITY FOR POSITIONING

1. We listen discursively in order to grasp what narrative is being created by our and others' utterances.
2. We listen to the plot of the narrative and thus to the positions it makes available.
3. We pay attention to how certain persons are placed in certain positions in the ongoing communication.
4. We converse in ways that create positions in stories that are inclusive and that help shape mutually respectful relationships.
5. We invite ourselves and others to engage in flexible positioning over time to expand the shared scope of possibilities.

INQUIRY OF VALUE TO THE WORK COMMUNITY

1. We act with attention to how our own and other people's positioning and contributions shape a social reality.
2. We strive to understand events in multiple perspectives.
3. We assess the moral quality of our own and others' action on its worth to the work community and its consequences for others (and not on the intentions).
4. We use an appreciative language to bring out the best in each other based on an awareness of how we co-create each other on an ongoing basis.
5. We contribute to generating participatory knowledge with a view to expanding everyone's body of experience and meaning-horizon.
6. We speak with others based on a conviction that they too are morally responsible and reliable from the point of view of their own position.

**THE OBLIGATION TO INTERACT
AS MORALLY RESPONSIBLE AGENTS**

1. We explain objectives and assumptions in the organization's development activities in order to enable everyone involved to consider whether they want to take part, how and to what extent.
2. We keep development and appraisal/evaluation separate in all the methods we use in the acknowledgement that they represent two incompatible contexts with separate sets of ground rules.
3. We contribute to negotiating and creating a shared understanding of the embeddedness of power in relationships and of the moral obligations and entitlements that should apply in the given situation.
4. We collaborate in the ongoing negotiation of reality as morally responsible agents.

The relational ethics flower grew out of social constructionism and its key idea that we construct our social reality through language and communication. Moral obligations and entitlements based on realism would look very different. In realism it is an important notion that we use language to describe and uncover an unambiguous reality. In extension of this assumption we would arrive at obligations such as "telling the truth", "speaking one's mind to others whether invited or uninvited", "providing feedback to others about their blind spots", etc. Realism also implies the idea of the person as an isolated individual who acts on the basis of inner drivers such as personality, motivation and emotions. This notion goes hand in hand with the discourse on the necessity of personal development, which makes it a moral obligation to introspect and strive to actualize one's potential. These examples of moral obligations that spring from realism do nothing to promote mutual relatedness in organizations.

REFLECTIONS

As authors, we hope this book can inspire others to notice and create better possibilities of action. This book can certainly not stand alone. Therefore we hope that many others will continue to develop the ideas and share their experiences and practical wisdom. There are also themes that are only tentatively outlined in this book, which we think deserve greater attention in the future from managers, consultants, employees, organizational theorists and students. Parenthetically, master's dissertations and other high-level dissertations often make important contributions to innovation in the area. We have chosen five areas that we think hold particular promise:

1. Continued efforts to assess the usefulness of widespread implicit assumptions about learning, development and the production of results

In this book we have explored the implicit assumptions in a number of familiar and widely accepted discourses, for example, assumptions about personal development as the path to becoming a better functioning member of the organization. It also includes the assumptions behind written versions of general ethical guidelines with examples from the world of research (Chapter 4). We also looked at the implicit assumptions behind organizational studies of problems and the discourse on individual dysfunction in the workplace (Chapter 5), and we have put into words the implicit assumptions about learning and the minimization of errors in a system for reporting errors in the health care system (Chapter 5).

Implicit assumptions form the basis of many of the methods and systems that have been developed within management and HR. The assumptions about the necessity of personal development and needs satisfaction, for example, lead to feedback exercises about a person's blind spots, 360-degree management appraisals and job satisfaction surveys.

The implicit assumptions about the usefulness of organizational surveys and studies of problems lead to workplace assessments, workplace climate surveys, long-term sickness review meetings, and formal HR policies in a growing number of areas (health policies, smoking policies, violence prevention policies, etc.).

The implicit assumptions about learning in a system for reporting errors in relation to preventing unintended events in the health care system lead to the development of systems for reporting errors, statistical analyses and the development of guidelines.

We do not doubt the good intentions behind these efforts. The methods and systems rest on the firm conviction that they will produce results in the form of more individual and shared learning, fewer errors, bigger and better work efforts, and higher efficiency.

But what if the assumptions are flawed? A first step in assessing the quality of the assumptions is to make the implicit assumptions explicit. Our book is one contribution. Only when the implicit assumptions have been put into words can we discuss them properly and review them critically. We conclude that these assumptions are unlikely to prove valid. The intentions are good, but the application of the methods and systems does not produce more and better possibilities of action – neither with regard to the achievement of results nor in regard to relational ethics.

In the future we should subject all our methods and activities to a thorough review process. That applies both to the wide range of methods that are used by HR departments to improve learning, development and results and to the forms of communication and conversation that managers and employees use in everyday life in organizations. We have presented an alternative range of assumptions that can serve as the basis for discovering more appreciative and relational methods for generating greater job satisfaction and better results in organizations (Chapter 6). In recent years we have been pleased to note a growing interest in many organizations – in HR departments as well as management – in pursuing dialogic and relational approaches that enable us to escape individualization, stigmatization of individuals, blame games, and a view of employees as victims and managers as villains. In many HR departments this interest is reflected in concrete efforts to rethink methods and in managers' demand for consultancy services that are based on appreciative and relational approaches.

2. Developing discourses and narratives that expand the scope of possibilities

Most of the discourses we have addressed in this book are characterized by low quality in the sense that they make few positions available, that the positions they do offer are predominantly negatively charged, and that it is difficult to escape a position once one has been placed in it, voluntarily or not. That applies both to the discourse on change management, the discourse on bullying and sexual harassment, and the discourse on documentation and evaluation. Once the discourses are practiced, the involved parties' scope of possibilities is restricted, and subject-object relationships are created in which some of the positioned individuals are denied the right to be met as responsible and reliable moral agents.

We have wondered about the widespread occurrence and popularity of these discourses – and it has been disheartening to see that many in the helping professions (such as psychology) contribute with great authority to cement these discourses as "scientific" ways of defining reality.

Meanwhile, it is difficult to find good examples of expansive and promising discourses and narratives that influence life in organizations. There are some, and we need many more. In Appreciative Inquiry the metaphor of a "journey of discovery" is used in reference to the joint efforts in an organization to create useful participatory knowledge, and the metaphor "the fifth province" is used about dialogic conversations in which the participants attempt to bridge the gap of major differences, disagreement and conflict. The image of "the fifth province" comes from old Irish legends in which it signified a place where the warring Irish chieftains could meet after having laid down their arms. It served as a place of asylum or refuge where the chieftains could focus on reaching a common understanding through communication. Inside "the fifth province" disagreement and differences were welcomed, and the merit of the various points of view was tested in the group. This metaphor is used in many organizations to frame situations and define ground rules for an open-minded and unprejudiced dialogue.

3. Increased respect for management and managers as contributors and morally responsible agents

An unintended consequence of many of the assumptions and discourses we have discussed here is that managers are referred to with disrespect, both within individual organizations and in the debate in the public media. The assumption that the satisfaction of the individual employee's needs is a crucial and indispensable condition for his or her ability to be committed and efficient on the job has a number of unfortunate consequences. Firstly, the assumption makes it tempting to use methods that implicitly define the employee as a victim or worthy of pity if he or she is able to point to something with which he or she is not happy. In accordance with the worldview inherent in realism, the employee should be protected by anonymity so that this "weak" member of the organization can speak freely about how (dis)satisfied he or she is with various conditions in the organization. Secondly, the assumption positions the managers as providers. They are the ones who have to provide the employees with an optimal psychological working environment, a good work day, well-defined goals, and a clear vision of their future in the organization. When employees find conditions to be less than optimal, the inadequacies are easily defined as being the fault of management. The employees are invited to assume a waiting position with questions such as, "When are we going to get a good psychological work environment?", "When will we have the necessary resources?", "When will we have competent management?" and in extension of this often the question, "Why haven't we seen any improvement yet when management promised to fix the problem last year?"

This type of discourse is not helpful, as both employees and managers are denied the possibility of appearing as contributors to the work community and of being recognized as morally responsible agents with good reasons to do what they do.

Furthermore, this type of discourse always focuses on the satisfaction of the employee's needs – not the manager's needs. An interesting pattern emerges where regularly recurring surveys are used to rate, on the one hand, the employee's needs satisfaction and, on the other hand, the manager's conduct and personality. Managers are constantly under suspicion for not performing well enough and thus for failing their employees. This means that there is every reason for managers – especially in the public sector – to feel under constant attack. As we have argued, this trend has gone too far with all the measures in place to appraise, rate, and judge the individual manager, as if he or she were an isolated individual acting in a vacuum, unaffected by the actions of other organizational members.

What would happen if we abandoned the idea that satisfying employees' needs are a prerequisite for their dedication to the job and efficient work efforts? Many things would change. Thousands of man hours that are currently spent in organizations on employee satisfaction surveys, workplace climate surveys, workplace appraisals, etc. could instead be dedicated to the job itself and on engaging in direct dialogue about how managers and employees contribute to the joint effort of achieving high-quality performance and helping each other succeed. That would be a better approach to learning about the actions and events that produce the best results.

We need new approaches to understanding management as a co-created phenomenon where managers and employees meet – from different positions and vantage points and with different opportunities of defining reality – as contributors worthy of respect and as morally responsible and reliable partners.

4. Intercultural communication

In this book we have demonstrated the potential complexity and unpredictability of the efforts to coordinate one's actions with those of others. Successful speech acts and effective interactions require in-depth knowledge of the culturally shaped norms and ground rules. That is a form of practical wisdom that cannot be acquired by studying textbooks or the company's HR policy manuals.

Nevertheless, there are huge amounts of tacit knowledge in organizations about the ethical aspects of everyday events. Much of this tacit knowledge is very difficult to put into words – even for organizational members from the majority culture. As long as this knowledge remains implicit it is difficult to help new employees from a minority culture background to fit in, as managers and employees from the majority culture are unable to explain the ethical ground rules. This is the case, until someone fails to respect these unwritten rules. When one's own ethical position is difficult to put into words, it becomes a substantial challenge to meet people from a different cultural background in an open-minded, curious and explorative manner that seeks to discover what their ethical framework looks like and how we can co-construct shared meaning.

Unfortunately, that is a topic we have only been able to touch upon very lightly within the frames of this book. We hope that others will take it up. In the current public debate in Denmark a hot topic is the demand that organizational members from non-Danish ethnic groups must learn to live in Danish culture. We would like to take a broader view: If Danish organizations wish to be able to attract and retain managers and employees from minority culture backgrounds they need to put in an effort to enable all employees to learn more about how to bridge the gap between different worldviews in everyday interactions. In this effort, some of the moral obligations and entitlements we have discussed above take on particular importance. For example, it is essential to be able to maneuver – and remain – within the field of tension between exposing oneself to other people's points of view and holding onto one's own moral point of view, especially in situations characterized by major differences and disagreement. Another important point is to interact with others based on the conviction that they are morally responsible and reliable as seen from their own position.

5. The major challenge of learning to practice relational ethics

Many organizations have difficulties attracting and retaining competent employees. We doubt that promises of "great opportunities for personal development" will hold much appeal in the future, but we are convinced that the overall ability of an organization to use appreciative communication in everyday interactions and to shape respectful relationships will be important in the long run. Future managers and employees will demand a high level of moral conduct in organizations, also in relation to everyday events and interactions. That makes it essential to learn more about how to practice relational ethics in order to move on from the complacency of good intentions to more and better possibilities of action aimed at shaping a desirable future.

We are convinced that it is possible to learn to practice relational ethics in organizations. It involves heightening our awareness of the moral aspects of everyday events, training our appreciative eye, developing our capacity for good judgment in specific situations, making room for a multitude of voices and perspectives, and assuming responsibility for our role as co-creators of each other and of each other's conditions for success. We hope that this book will contribute to the development of a richer language about morality and ethics that can help make moral dilemmas a shared endeavor in organizations. We also hope that this book has helped make the reader increasingly aware of his or her own practical wisdom about morality and ethics. Finally, we hope to have sown some seeds for perspectives and topics that many others will cultivate, and we look forward to seeing the results in buds and in bloom.

ABOUT THE AUTHORS

 ## GITTE HASLEBO

Gitte Haslebo, Master's Degree in Social Psychology from the University of Kansas and Master of Science in Psychology from the University of Copenhagen. Gitte is a certified specialist and supervisor in organisational psychology.

She established the consultancy firm in 1991 and carries out consultancy and training tasks both for private and public companies in Denmark and Norway. The tasks comprise consultancy assignments in periods of change, conflict dissolution, leadership and organizational development, training of managers, training courses in consultancy and coaching, coaching of managers and managerial groups and professional support and advice in managerial crises.

The work is based on social constructionism and inspired by systemic, appreciative and narrative approaches to consultation, management and organizational development.

She is the author and co-author of numerous books and articles on leadership and organisational development. Some of the articles have been translated into English and can be found on the web page www.haslebo-partnere.dk. One of the books was published by Karnac Books in 2000: Haslebo, G. and Nielsen, K. S. *Systems and Meaning. Consulting in Organizations.*

For years she has worked as a board member of the Danish

Psychological Publishing agency and was appointed an associate to TAOS Institute in 2008.

Owner and Chief Consultant at Haslebo & Partnere, Copenhagen and Ribe, Denmark.

Email: gh@haslebo-partnere.dk

www.haslebo-partnere.dk

MAJA LOUA HASLEBO

Maja Loua Haslebo, Master of Science in Psychology from the University of Copenhagen (2004) and Bachelor of Science in Psychology (Honors) from the University of Westminster, London (2000).

As an organizational consultant at Haslebo & Partners, Copenhagen, Denmark, Maja Loua Haslebo works with development of leadership, commitment, followership and cooperation through systemic, appreciative and narrative approaches. Maja works as a process consultant, coach, and strategic partner for leaders, managers, and HR consultants in connection with leadership and organizational development, as well as development of HR-tools. Maja also teaches in Haslebo & Partners' educations and training programs.

Furthermore, Maja is an editor of the electronic magazine on constructionist leadership and consultancy work: Relational Practice. This magazine comes out four times a year and can be downloaded for free at www.relationelpraksis.dk. The articles are written by organizational members who are inspired by social constructionist thinking and have applied this to their work with leadership and organizational development.

Previously, Maja worked as a business consultant at CfL: Danish Centre for Leadership.

Maja Loua Haslebo has authored and co-authored a large number of articles, essays and books on leadership development, consultancy work and organizational development in a social constructionist perspective.

Email: mlh@haslebo-partnere.dk, www.haslebo-partnere.dk

REFERENCES

> Austin, J. L. (1962): *How to do Things with Words.* New York: Oxford University Press.

> Barge, K.J. & Pearce, B. W. (2004): A reconnaissance of CMM research. *Human Systems: The Journal of Systemic Consultation & Management,* *15*, pp. 13-32.

> Berger, P. L. & Luckmann, T. (1966): *The Social Construction of Reality.* New York: Anchor Books.

> Barrett, F. & Fry, R, (2005) *Appreciative Inquiry: A Positive Approach to Building Cooperative Capacity.* Chagrin Falls, OH: Taos Institute Publications.

> Bruner, J. (1990): *Acts of Meaning.* Cambridge: Harvard University Press.

> Burr, V. (1999): *An Introduction to Social Constructionism.* London: Routledge.

> Campbell, D. (2000): *The Socially Constructed Organization.* London & New York: Karnac Books.

> Campbell, D. & Groenbaek, M. (2006): *Taking Positions in the Organization.* London and New York: H. Karnac Books.

> Cooperrider, D. L. (1999): Positive image, positive action: The affirmative basis of organizing. In: Srivastva, S. & Cooperrider, D. L. (Eds.), *Appreciative Management and Leadership.* San Francisco: Jossey-Bass, pp. 91-125.

> Cooperrider, D. L. & Srivastva, S. (1987): Appreciative inquiry in organisational life. *Research in Organizational Change and Development, 1,* 129-169.

> Cooperrider, D. L. & Srivasta, S. (1999): Appreciative inquiry in organizational life. In: Srivastva, S. & Cooperrider, D. L. (Eds.), *Appreciative Management and Leadership*. San Francisco: Jossey-Bass, pp. 401-442.

> Cooperrider, D. & Whitney, D. (2001): A positive revolution in change: Appreciative Inquiry. In: Cooperrider, D. et al. (Eds.), *Appreciative Inquiry. An Emerging Direction for Organization Development*. Champaign, Illinois: Stipes Publishing, pp. 5-29.

> Cronen, V. E. (1995): Coordinated Management of Meaning: The consequentiality of communication and the recapturing of experience. In: Sigman, S. J. (Ed.), *The Consequentiality of Communication*. Mahwah, NJ: Lawrence Erlbaum Associates, pp. 17-65.

> Cronen, V. & Lang, P. (1994): Language and action: Wittgenstein and Dewey in the practice of therapy and consultation. *Human Systems, 5*: 5-43.

> Dansk Selskab for Patientsikkerhed (2010): *Act on Patient Safety in the Danish Health Care System. ACT No. 429 of 10/06/2003*.

> Davies, B. and Harré, R. (1990): Positioning: The discursive production of selves. *Journal for the theory of social behaviour, 20*, 43-63.

> Dewey, J. (1891): Moral theory and practice. *International Journal of Ethics, 1*, 186-203.

> Dewey, J. (1916): *Democracy and Education*. New York: The Free Press (this edition 1966).

> Dewey, J. (1925, later edition 1958): *Experience and Nature*. Chicago: Open Court.

> Dewey, J. (1929): *The Quest for Certainty*. New York: Capricorn Books (this edition 1960).

> Dewey, J. (1938): *Logic: The Theory of Inquiry*. New York: Henry Holt & Co.

> Dewey, J. & Tufts, J. H. (1909): *Ethics*. New York: Henry Holt and Co.

> Dreyfus, H. L. & Rabinow, P. (1983): *Michael Foucault. Beyond Structuralism and Hermeneutics*. Chicago: The University of Chicago Press.

> Foucault, M. (1970): *The Order of Things: An Archaeology of the Human Sciences*. New York: Random House.

> Foucault, M. (1980): *The History of Sexuality. Volume 1. An Introduction*. (Translated by Robert Hurley). New York: Vintage/Random House.

> Foucault, M. (1983). The Subject and Power. Afterword. In: Dreyfus, H.L. & Rabinow, P. (Eds.), *Michel Foucault. Beyond Structuralism and Hermeneutics*. Chicago: The University of Chicago Press, second edition, pp. 208-226.

> Foucault, M. (1994): *Ethics: The Essential Works, 1*. London: Penguin Press.

> Freedman, J. & Combs, G. (1996): *Narrative Therapy. The Social Construction of Preferred Realities*. New York: W.W. Norton & Company.

> Gergen, K. J. (1985): Social constructionist inquiry: Context and implications. In: Gergen, K. J. & Davis, K. (Eds.), *The Social Construction of the Person*. New York: Springer Verlag, pp. 3-18.

> Gergen, K. J. (1994): *Realities and Relationships. Soundings in Social Construction*. Cambridge, MA: Harvard University Press.

> Gergen, K. J. & Gergen, M. (2004): *Social Construction – Entering the Dialogue*. Chagrin Falls, Ohio: Taos Institute Publications.

> Groes, J. & Haslebo, G. (2005): Personlig afvikling. *Politiken*, 12 July.

> Hammond, S.A. (1996): *The Thin Book of Appreciative Inquiry*. Plano, TX: CSS Publishing Co.

> Hare, R. M. (1981): *Moral Thinking.* Oxford: Oxford University Press.

> Harré, R. (Ed.), (1986): *The Social Construction of Emotions.* Great Britain: Basil Blackwell.

> Harré, R. & Parrott, W. G. (1996): *The Emotions. Social, Cultural and Biological Dimensions.* London: Sage Publications.

> Harré, R. & Moghaddam, F. (2003): Introduction: The self and others in traditional psychology and in positioning theory. In: Harré, R. & Moghaddam, F. (Eds.), *The Self and Others. Positioning Individuals and Groups in Personal, Political and Cultural Contexts.* United States: Praeger Publishers, pp. 1-11.

> Haslebo, G. & Nielsen, K. S. (2000): *Systems and Meaning. Consulting in Organizations.* London and New York: H. Karnac Books.

> Haslebo, G. (2003): *Positioning – applying the narrative approach to consultancy work in organizations.* www.haslebo-partnere.dk. (The article was first published in Danish with the title: Positionsskift og erkendelse i organisationer – inspiration fra den narrative tilgang. *Erhvervspsykologi, 1,* 54-67).

> Haslebo, G. (2004): *Relationer i Organisationer – en Verden til Forskel.* Virum: Dansk psykologisk Forlag. (The book has only been published in Danish. The title means: *Relationships in organizations – a world of difference).*

> Heede, D. (2004): *Det Tomme Menneske. Introduktion til Michel Foucault.* Copenhagen: Museum Tusculanums Forlag.

> Holmgren, A. (2004): Saying, doing and making: teaching CMM theory. *Human Systems: The Journal of Systemic Consultation & Management. 15,* issues 1-3, 89-100.

> Honneth, A. (1995): *The Struggle for Recognition: The Moral Grammar of Social Conflicts.* Cambridge, MA: The MIT Press.

> Honneth, A. (2001): Invisibility: On the Epistemology of "Recognition". In: *The Aristotelian Society*, Bristol, Supplementary Volume LXXV, pp. 111-126.

> Honneth, A. (2007): *Disrespect: The Normative Foundations of Critical Theory.* Cambridge, UK: Polity Press.

> Hosking, D. M. (2006): Organizations, organizing and related concepts of change. In: Hosking, D. M. & McNamee, S. (Eds.), *The Social Construction of Organization.* Sweden and Norway: Liber & Copenhagen Business School Press, pp. 54-68.

> Hosking, D. M. and McNamee, S. (2006): Subject-Object relations, knowledge and power. In: Hosking, D. M. & McNamee, S. (Eds.), *The Social Construction of Organization.* Sweden and Norway: Liber & Copenhagen Business School Press, pp. 86-90.

> Jensen, M. B. & Jespersen, K.(2005): *Det er menneskeligt at fejle – og at lære. En undersøgelse af systemet for rapportering af utilsigtede hændelser som læringstiltag i det danske sygehusvæsen.* Master's dissertation. Department of Psychology. University of Copenhagen.

> Kanter, R. M. (1996): *The Change Masters: The Corporate Entrepreneurs at Work.* London: International Thomson Business Press.

> Kotter, J. (1996): *Leading Change.* Boston, MA: Harvard Business School Press.

> Laird, J. D. & Apostoleris, H. (1996): Emotional self-control and self-perception: Feelings are the solution, not the problem. In: Harré, R. & Parrott, W. G. (Eds.), *The Emotions. Social, Cultural and Biological Dimensions.* London: Sage Publications, pp. 285-301.

> Lakoff, G. & Johnson, M. (1980): *Metaphors We Live By.* Chicago: University of Chicago Press.

> Larsen, H.H. (2006): *Human Resource Management. Licence to work: Arbejdslivets tryllestov eller håndjern?* Copenhagen: Forlaget Valmuen. Loughlin, M. (2002): *Ethics, Management and Mythology – Rational Decision Making for Health Service Professionals.* Oxford: Radcliffe Medical Press Ltd.

> MacIntyre, A. (1981): *After Virtue – a Study in Moral Theory.* London: Duckworth.

> Martin, L. H., Gutman, H. & Hutton, P. H. (1998): *Technologies Of The Self – A Seminar With Michael Foucault.* Amherst: The University of Massachusetts Press.

> Mattingly, C. (2005): Toward a vulnerable ethics of research practice. *Health: The Interdisciplinary Journal for Social Study of Health, Illness and Medicine. 9*, 453-471.

> McNamee, S. & Gergen, K. J. (1999): *Relational Responsibility: Resources for Sustainable Dialogue.* Thousand Oaks, CA: Sage Publications.

> Milgram, S. (1997): *Obedience to Authority: An Experimental View.* New York: Harper & Row.

> Mishler, E. G. (2005): Patient stories, narratives of resistance and the ethics of humane care: a la recherché du temps perdu. *Health: The Interdisciplinary Journal for Social Study of Health, Illness and Medicine. 9*, 431-451.

> Monk, G., Winslade, J., Crocket, K. & Epston, D. (Eds.) (1997): *Narrative Therapy in Practice – The Archaeology of Hope*, San Francisco: Jossey-Bass Publishers.

> Oliver, C. (2005): *Reflexive Inquiry - A Framework for Consultancy Practice.* London: Karnac Books.

Parrott, G. W. (2003): Positioning and the emotions. In: Harré, R. & Moghaddam, F. (Eds.), *The Self and Others. Positioning Individuals and Groups in Personal, Political and Cultural Contexts*. New York: Praeger Publishers, pp. 29-43.

Pearce, W.B. (1976): The Coordinated Management of Meaning: A rules-based theory of interpersonal communication. In: Miller, G. R. (Ed.). *Explorations in Interpersonal Communication*. Beverly Hills, California: Sage, pp.17-36.

Pearce, W. B. (1994): *Interpersonal Communication: Making Social Worlds*. New York: Harper Collins.

Pearce, W.B. (2007a) *Kommunikation og Skabelsen af Sociale Verdener*. Copenhagen: Dansk psykologisk Forlag.

Pearce, W.B. (2007b): *Making Social Worlds. A Communication Perspective*. Oxford: Blackwell Publishing.

Pearce, W. B. & Cronen, V.E. (1980): *Communication, Action and Meaning*. New York: Praeger.

Pearce, W.B. & Kearney, J (Eds.). (2004): Special Issue, Coordinated Management of Meaning: Extensions and applications. *Human Systems. The Journal of Systemic Consultation and Management, 15, issues 1-3*.

Pearce, W. B. & Littlejohn, S.W (1997): *Moral Conflict – When Social Worlds Collide*. Thousand Oaks, CA: Sage Publications.

Ricoeur, P. (2006): *On Translation*. London and New York: Routledge.

Riessman, C. K. (2005): Exporting ethics: a Narrative about narrative research in South India. *Health: The Interdisciplinary Journal for Social Study of Health, Illness and Medicine. 9*, 473-490.

> Riessman, C. K. & Mattingly, C. (2005): Introduction: toward a context-based ethics for social research in health. *Health: The Interdisciplinary Journal for Social Study of Health, Illness and Medicine. 9*, 427-429.

> Rose, N. (1999): *Governing the Soul. The Shaping of the Private Self.* (2nd edition). London: Free Association Books.

> Scheuer, J. (1998): *Den Umulige Samtale - Sprog, køn og Magt i Jobsamtaler.* Viborg: Akademisk Forlag.

> Schiøler, T. et al. (2001) Forekomsten af utilsigtede hændelser på sygehuse – en retrospektiv gennemgang af journaler. *Ugeskrift for læger,* 163 (38) 5370-5378.

> Shailor, J. G. The meaning and use of "context" in the theory of the Coordinated Management of Meaning. In: Owen, J. L. (Ed.), *Context and Communication Behavior.* Reno, Nevada: Context Press, pp. 97-110.

> Sigman, S. J. (1995): Introduction. Toward study of consequentiality (Not consequenses) of communication. In: Sigman, S. J. (Ed.), *The Consequentiality of Communication.* Mahwah, NJ: Lawrence Erlbaum, pp.1-14.

> Stewart, J. & Zediker, K. E. (2002): Dialogue as tensional ethical practice. *Southern Californian Communication Journal,* 2/3, 224-242.

> Sundhedsstyrelsen (2005): *Orientering fra medicinaldirektøren.* Sundhedsstyrelsens Nyhedsbrev, 3 April. (Newsletter from the Danish National Board of Health).

> Waldron, V. R. (2000): Relational experiences and emotion at work. In: Fineman, S. (Ed.), *Emotion in Organizations.* London: Sage publications, pp. 64-82.

> Watzlawick, P., Beavin, J. H. & Jackson, D.D. (1967): *The Pragmatics of Human Communication: A Study of Interactional Patterns, Pathologies and Paradoxes.* New York: W.W. Norton.

> White, M. (2002): Addressing personal failure. *The International Journal of Narrative Therapy and Community Work. 3,* 33-76.

> White, M. & Epston, D. (1990): *Narrative Means to Therapeutic Ends.* New York: Norton.

> Whittaker, E. (2005): Adjudicating entitlements: The emerging discourses of research ethics boards. *Health: The Interdisciplinary Journal for Social Study of Health, Illness and Medicine. 9,* 513-535.

> Winslade, J. & Monk, G. (2001): *Narrative Mediation. A New Approach to Conflict Resolution.* San Francisco: John Wiley.

> Wittgenstein, L. (1953): *Philosophical Investigations.* (Trans. G. Anscombe). New York: Macmillan.

CPSIA information can be obtained at www.ICGtesting.com
Printed in the USA
BVOW040739060112

279877BV00001B/98/P